God

Revised Edition

God

Revised Edition

Amy Welborn

Our Sunday Visitor Publishing Division
Our Sunday Visitor, Inc.
Huntington, IN 46750

Nihil Obstat
Msgr. Michael Heintz, Ph.D.
Censor Librorum

Imprimatur
✠ Kevin C. Rhoades, Bishop of Fort Wayne-South Bend
July 20, 2010

The *Nihil Obstat* and *Imprimatur* are official declarations that a book or pamphlet is free of doctrinal or moral error. No implication is contained therein that those who have granted the *Nihil Obstat* or *Imprimatur* agree with the contents, opinions, or statements expressed.

ISBN: 978-1-59276-683-3 (Inventory No. T962)
LCCN: 2010928872

Cover design by Amanda Falk
Cover photo: Think Stock
Interior art by JDA Studio
Interior design by Sherri L. Hoffman

PRINTED IN THE UNITED STATES OF AMERICA

To all my students, who asked the questions,
and
to Michael, who told me,
"The answer is 'yes.'"

Contents

CHAPTER 1

On the Spot

IT'S HAPPENED TO you. Don't deny it, and don't be ashamed. Just ease into it.

Can you remember where you were at the time? Sitting in the cafeteria counting French fries? Meditating on an exceptionally stubborn geometry proof? Wondering how your friend trapped you into helping her supervise her little sister's sleepover party?

So you're sitting there, minding your own business, when you sense a turn in the conversation around you. The tone shifts. It's getting just a little more intense in here, and it's not the geometry or the cafeteria food or even the Wii competition downstairs.

It hits you. God's in the room. Right . . . here.

"Hey, " someone says.

Why is everyone looking at me?

"Don't you go to church?"

Oh. That's why.

"So you must believe in God, right?"

"I guess. Sure."

It's only a matter of time now . . .

"Why do you believe in God?"

Yup. Here we go.

Yes, here you go. Ten years of religious education in some form or another, a jillion Sundays in church, and thousands of minutes spent listening to people talk about God, ripe and ready to be used in this exciting world of heady, exhilarating, real-live philosophical discussions. Why do you believe in God? Are your friends ready? Can they handle it?

"Uh — kind of hard to say. I just do, I guess."

Awesome. John the Baptist, watch out.

Oh. So . . . it didn't exactly turn out well? They weren't stunned into awestruck silence? They just kept on peppering you with questions about "proof" and science and how could a good God let people suffer and how can religious people do the bad things they do?

Isn't it awful to be asked to explain something you know is true, but just can't explain?

Awkward!

It's not that you haven't thought about that whole God thing. A lot. It's just that it's such a challenge to talk about, isn't it?

First of all, it's personal. Really personal. Your beliefs make perfect sense to you (most of the time), but it's hard to get it across to people who haven't lived your particular life of joy and pain or know what it's like to marvel at answered prayers.

Besides, you know you owe your questioners more than that, anyway. They wouldn't be talking or even thinking about it if they didn't want to know for sure if there really is a God, something or someone solidly true for everyone, all the time.

Yes, sharing your feelings about how connected you felt to God when you sat on the big rock on the edge of the Grand Canyon, or the other night under the stars, is very nice and might make a great poem someday, but it misses the point, just like telling someone how awesome it felt to finish your pre-calculus problems doesn't answer their questions about the homework:

"So — what *are* the answers? And how did you get them?"

Well, *is* there an answer? To the God stuff. Is there a way to talk about it that goes beyond personal feelings?

After all, thousands of books have been written about God. Are they just filled with someone saying, "I dunno, I just do," or "It's what my parents taught me" over and over again through hundreds of pages? Lots of very smart people believe in God and have given their lives to Him and for Him. Would they do all that for something less than truth, for nothing more than fuzzy, hopeful feelings? Is that worth dying for? Is it even worth hauling your tail out of bed in the morning and going to church for?

To the Rescue...

I have news. Really, really big news. *Good news.* You might not have heard it, though. Ready?

On the Spot

You are not the only person in the history of the world who has wondered about God.

One other thing: The guy at your table with his elbow in the nachos is not the first person who's tried to figure out how a good God and suffering children somehow all fits together.

You are not the only person in the history of Christianity to have a heart-stopping moment of existential cosmic panic in which you think, "What if it's all made up after all? What if it's not true?"

In the almost 2,000 years since Christianity began, during the past four thousand years of Jewish history, and even, really, since human beings have been able to think, period, there have actually been people who have pondered faith. They've grappled with the same questions and fundamental choices you have: Life or darkness? Meaning or chaos? God or nothing at all?

And some of them came up with answers.

And they wrote them down.

And they still make sense.

Not kidding.

I'm not surprised at your surprise. After all, you've grown up in a culture that doesn't discuss ideas at all, much less ideas about religion. We just don't see back further than last week, much less back to the many interesting and wise things people hundreds of years ago had to say. If you are like a lot of the young people I have known and taught, you might also have the sneaking suspicion that your religious education hasn't always, every minute, been the greatest help here.

You've had decent teachers. Maybe even some great ones. But if you're like many kids, you might have been struck by the fact that when it comes to religious knowledge, adults have very low expectations of what kids should or even could know. Kids have often wondered out loud to me why it is that the most challenging religious reflection expected of a sixteen-year-old who can drive,

hold a job, design a web page, balance chemical equations, and study *Hamlet* is constructing a collage about "The Beatitudes in Today's World." They've wondered why their other texts are so big and solid, while their religion books tend to be flimsy things filled with the reflection question and lots of pictures of birds, meadows, and rainbows. They can't help but compare and can't help but wonder what's being communicated to them about how seriously they're supposed to take religion after all.

So there it is. You live in a time when the pressure to explain your faith is pretty intense, and the conditions in which you're asked to do this explaining can be unsympathetic. Hostile, even. Books preaching atheism and the evils of religion are regular bestsellers these days. And then, to bring the whole mess to a simply stunningly frustrating conclusion, hardly anyone is giving you clear, solid help in dealing with all of these really important questions that you and your friends are asking.

Here's what I'm trying to do in this book. I want to share some of those interesting, well-pondered, and actually very useful answers about God's existence and nature with you in ways that are clear and relevant.

For surprise, surprise — not a single question an atheist or agnostic friend poses to you is new. Neither are those questions and doubts that pop into your own head, which might be pretty comforting to realize. For all of these questions we'll be talking about — they're not just questions *other* people have. They're your questions, too. They're your doubts. And no, doubt isn't a dirty word, even among people of faith. Doubts and questions are real. Pursuing the answers helps us deepen our faith. They can bring us closer to other people, because we can better understand where they're coming from. They can also bring us closer to God.

Do you know the story of Job? You probably know bits and pieces of it — that Job suffered a lot, for apparently no reason. You may have heard the saying about the "patience of Job."

Well, that is a weird saying for one reason: Job *wasn't* patient. He lost all his wealth, his family was all killed, and he was struck with a hideous disease, and he couldn't help but wonder why.

His friends came and comforted him by telling him that he must have done something wrong to deserve all this pain. Some comfort, huh?

Job wouldn't take it, though. He argued that even though sure, he was a sinner, there was really nothing he'd done in his life that would make him deserve *this* much punishment. And so he went right to the source with his questions: he went to God.

Now God's answers to Job are very well known, and you might have even read them in literature class. God responds to Job, essentially, that there is a huge mystery in life, but God has a plan, even though it may be murky to us.

I don't bring this up to talk about suffering — that comes later — but to help us think about doubts and questions.

Because in the end, God comes to one person in this story. Only one person has the awesome privilege of being in the very presence of God. And it's not the friends who gather round and tell Job not to ask questions. It's Job — with all of his questions, pain and confusion. He brings it all to God, honestly — and God is there.

So don't hide your own questions from yourself or, most importantly, from God.

Now, as this really ancient story of Job points out, these questions about God aren't new. Nor are the ideas that spring from the questions, the truths that people have come to about God. You are, to put it simply, not alone. There is a lot more to say about God than "He exists because I sure hope He does" and ways to talk about these matters that depend on more than feelings and are, once you start looking at them, pretty interesting, too.

Planting Seeds

As you read, try to remember one very important thing. When you discuss these issues with those who disagree with you, your goal really shouldn't be to "win," as tempting and even instinctive a reaction as that might be. Any intellectually plausible answers we can offer to tough questions about God brought to us by those who don't believe are only a beginning, for faith is about more than ideas.

> Let them at least learn what this religion is which they are attacking before attacking it.
> — Blaise Pascal, *Pensées*

It's a long way to faith, and your job is not to convert anyone — God does that part. You're being called to cooperate with the Spirit which has brought you and your friend together at this point to do what you can to open his or her mind to the idea that believing in God isn't crazy, and, when you look at reality as a whole, actually makes a lot of sense. You have to remember — you're not the Savior. Jesus is. Once you've done your best in helping open someone's mind to the idea of God, the journey takes a slightly different turn, and it becomes your job to pray that an open mind just might lead to an open heart, ready to accept God's love.

What you're going to find — I can almost guarantee it — is that once you sit down and start talking reasonably and knowledgeably about these questions, the problems your atheist or New Age friends have concerning God or religion aren't even part of what Christians believe. In other words, they're rejecting ideas that aren't really true — God is a vicious being who gleefully sends people to hell, or believing in God makes you an enemy of science, or believing in God means losing your

individuality — and that, of course, have nothing to do with the reality of God.

It's sort of like this: There's someone in your school whom you've never really met but about whom you've heard very interesting and terrible gossip. The gossip — she's two-faced, or he's nothing but a player — has defined that person in your mind, so you've decided she or he isn't anyone you'd ever want to know.

Then one day, you miss the bus and you're standing in front of the school, waiting for your mom, idly wondering just how mad she's going to be this time. You hear a backpack being dropped to the ground behind you. You turn around, and there's The Gossip. You've heard all these awful things and you decided a long time ago she was a lost cause, so you don't say hi.

But she does.

And she starts talking, wondering how irritated her brother is going to be today when he has to pick her up at school. You say something about your own dilemma and she laughs. You both laugh, talk about how great it will be to have your drivers' licenses and how much you're dreading exams.

> Not to have faith is not a personal fault, it is a misfortune.
> — Étienne Gilson, *The Philosopher and Theology*

It dawns on you that while people sure had a lot to say about this girl, hardly any of it was right, and you were wrong to base your judgment of her on other people's ignorance.

So that's the way it is. There's a lot of gossip out there about God. Most of it's wrong, ill-informed, and unthinking. I want to help you clear up that gossip — not just because it's incorrect but because when people buy into it, they're missing out on something that can deepen and even save their lives: getting to know a faithful, loving Friend.

CHAPTER 2

Truth or Consequences

"WHAT'S TRUE FOR you may not be true for me."

"One opinion is just as valuable as another. "

"Faith is good because it helps get you through hard times, but it doesn't matter *what* you believe in, as long as you believe in something."

"One religion is just as true as another."

Sound familiar? Probably. Sound reasonable? If nothing else, you have to admit, it's a pretty cagey way to end an uncomfortable discussion about what's true: suddenly declaring there's no such thing as truth. But if you take a second to think about the inevitable conclusion of those views: "Nothing's true, but everything's true, and it's all just opinion anyway" — the whole thing pretty much collapses in absurdity.

We're going to come back and take the scalpel to each of those assertions individually later in the chapter. Before we do that, though, let's talk about attitude.

For some reason, when we start in on conversations about truth and faith, we believers suddenly, almost always, snap into a defensive stance. You know how it feels. But does it have to be that way?

Of course not. When questioned on your faith, why immediately assume that *your* beliefs are the only ones in the room that need defending? Why not turn it around and ask the same of the person you're talking with? They'll want you to prove God exists. Can they prove He *doesn't*? They'll want you to explain how God could have created the universe. Can they explain how it came to exist *without* God?

Push. That's what this is about. Gently, yet firmly, push — not the people, but the arguments they're offering. Push so they can see those easy assertions about the impossibility of a God actually stand on pretty shaky ground. Push so they can see how contradictory some of their statements are. Push those arguments to their logical conclusions, and then see how they stand.

Telling the Truth . . . about Truth

Have you ever said anything that, if you were honest, you would have to admit that you didn't really believe?

Do you cringe when you remember the times you've shouted, "I hate you!" to a parent? Have you ever explained, in a frustrated rage, "No, I DON'T care if I don't break seven hundred on the SAT, can't bring my grades up, and then can't get into college, thank you very much. No, I DON'T want to do anything interesting or useful with my life! Where's the remote?" Do you ever wonder how in the world you got caught up with those other girls that day who were dissing your supposedly best friend behind her back and why you said the things you did, even if you knew they weren't true? Do you ever want to just go back in time and be struck with laryngitis the day you told that girl you only kind of liked that you really loved her?

Why do we say such stupid things?

The reasons are pretty simple:

- We get caught up in emotion, usually either anger or desire.
- We're proud. We don't want to admit that we're wrong, or we want to impress others.

- We haven't thought through the consequences of our words.

In general, while our rational brains know what we really think, we're willing to disconnect our mouths and emotions from it in order to get what we want at the moment: to be left alone, to inflict or avoid pain, to get another date, or to look cool.

To put it bluntly: we're selfish.

Now back to truth. I'm suggesting to you that when people try to close off discussion about God by announcing that nothing's really true anyway, so it's all not worth talking about, don't accept it. Call them on it. Push.

This might not be a point you have to explicitly bring out, and maybe you even shouldn't, but it's worth thinking about. You know how easy it is to say things we don't mean in order to get what we want? Could it just be that some people declare there's no truth, simply because, deep down, they don't want to face — the Truth?

> Truth is so obscure in these times, and falsehood so established, that, unless we love the truth, we cannot know it.
> — Blaise Pascal, *Pensées*

No Such Thing as Truth. And That's the Truth.

So step back from the religion talk for a minute and look at the whole idea of "truth" for a minute. What is "truth," anyway?

The Greek philosopher Plato (who lived a few hundred years before Christ) defined truth as "that which is." Pointing to a cat and calling it a rock isn't true, because the cat isn't a rock. Saying, "I love you" when you don't is a terrible, hurtful lie.

There are a couple of other words that will come in handy when you try to tease all of this apart. The first is "objective." To talk about "objective reality" or "objective truth" is to describe

things as they are, in and of themselves, without our opinions shading our description, just as an objective evaluation of you would attempt to describe you as you are, without regard to whether the person doing the evaluating liked you or not. The opposite of "objective" is "subjective." A subjective view on a matter incorporates our opinions.

Let's look at an example to sort out all of this. At this moment you might be sitting on an object with a back, a seat, and four legs. You're sitting on a chair. That's truth, and it's objective. It's not a table. It's not a mushroom or a mound of sea coral. Chair. You are sitting on a chair. Got it?

Now, you may be very impressed with the chair, thinking perhaps that it's positively the loveliest chair you've ever seen. You may be sitting there, hardly able to wait to get up so you can more closely examine the shiny metal legs, the intriguing form-fitting plastic seat, and its subtle, yet breathtakingly hypnotic gray color. However, the person next to you, as much as she can be moved to think about the stupid chair, might disagree, claiming it's the ugliest chair she's ever seen, and that you really need to get a life.

That's her opinion.

And you see, it really is. Objectively, it's a chair, and nothing can be done about it. Your subjective view is that it's a lovely chair, but your neighbor hates it. Fine. It's part of that whole realm of life in which our perceptions of value and beauty vary. We'd really be more accurate to call them preferences rather than different views of truth. Vanilla or chocolate? Lima beans, Brussels sprouts, or neither, ever again? Jeans or dresses? Buzz cut or mullet? Ankle tat or belly? Preferences. Opinions. No right answer.

But is the whole of life — every single part — really that way? The way some talk, you'd think it was — that it's impossible, and maybe even impolite, to try to say anything definitive about

It's a **ROCK!!**

anything. That there's no such thing as objective truth; all opinions about the nature of everything — not just chairs, but morals and God included — are equally true.

> Thirst was made for water; inquiry for truth.
> — C. S. Lewis, *The Great Divorce*

It's a common way to weasel out of discussions about religion, God, and morality: to say that what anyone and everyone believes is equally true. Then we can retreat into our little shells, believe what we want, not worry about what other people believe, and surely not ever, ever judge them. Because nothing's false, anyway, so how can you?

Once again, so easy to say, but does anyone — I mean anyone — really believe it?

True Enough

No, they don't. No matter what they say, they don't. What you're trying to do here is difficult, but still pretty straightforward. You're trying to help your friend see that truth exists, she really does believe that it's so, and that the existence of God falls in *that* category, not the one about hairstyles and music.

So start at a really basic level: people, places, and things. Truth exists there, right? We know that the National Football League exists and that dogs bark. They know that Franklin Delano Roosevelt was a president of the United States seventy years ago, and not now. Easy, right?

Okay, now move beyond that pretty obvious point. What about things that aren't so concrete, like shared values? Is there really no basis on which to judge other people's actions as right or wrong? Are values really just opinions and nothing more, interchangeable, all equally "true?"

If you want to know, just ask. The next time you're in a discussion about truth and values, and Mr. Relativist tries to cop out with the declaration that there's no such thing as truth anyway, try the following arguments.

1. Hey, I really like your car. It's mine now. No? But I thought my opinion was as valuable as yours. I thought there was no such thing as truth. If that's so, then your idea that there is such a thing as "personal property" is nothing more than opinion and has no more value than mine. Keys, please.

2. Oh, absolutely. I agree. Anyone who believes that moral values have an objective basis and apply equally to everyone is a subhuman piece of trash who shouldn't be allowed to vote, drive cars, or eat anything but uncooked barley and peach pits. You don't think so? Why not? Because it wouldn't be . . . right? Because it's not . . . right . . . to treat human beings that way? But I thought . . . oh, never mind.

3. Did you hear? Quentin Tarantino asked me to work on his next movie! What? You don't believe me? You think that what I'm saying is . . . not true? But I thought you didn't believe in truth. You don't have the right to judge whether what I'm saying is true or not . . . because you don't believe in truth.

Pretty absurd. Now try this on.

You say that there's no such thing as objective truth that's true for everyone, all the time. Do you believe that that statement is true for everyone, all the time, that there's no such thing as objective truth? How can that be?

How can you make a statement about what's objectively true for everyone if you don't believe that anything is true for everyone all the time?

So what's the point? It's to help you dismantle, right from the start, a basic premise you'll encounter: the attempt to undercut what you have to share about God by claiming that there's no truth anyway, and therefore, no God for everyone.

In using the examples I've given, and others like them that you can think of yourself, you can help the people you're talking with see that they do, indeed, believe in objective truth. They believe that the world is round and that it's always wrong to abuse a child. They believe that they exist. They believe and live out of the concept of truth.

Your goal at this point is to move the discussion just a little further down the road. Not the whole way yet, but just to the point where everyone can agree that the existence of things isn't dependent on our opinion or perceptions. Mosquitoes exist whether we want them to or not. So do the concepts of truth, and right and wrong. Some of us may glibly say that these last two are relative concepts, but we honestly don't live as though they are, and when we actually try, we almost always have a motive that's well served by denying the existence of truth or moral values. Could it be the same for our thoughts on God?

Finally, it's always helpful to be brutally logical.

Look, you say. You can go on all you want about the spiritual realm or the mysteries of the universe, but the fact is, either a thing exists or it doesn't. It is simply not possible that God both exists and doesn't.

I don't care how much of an easy, squishy out it seems, we have got to get real about this. You either went to school today or you didn't. This book exists or it doesn't. It can't be either, and it can't be both.

So it is with God. Either God exists, created the universe, and continues to sustain it, or there is no God, anywhere, of any sort. The universe can't be both created by God and not created by God. It can't be either, and it can't be both.

So now what do we do? We've inched our way towards accepting that maybe, when we talk about what is and isn't, we can, indeed, talk about God. There are a lot of obstacles on the way: our limited perceptions, our subjective desires about who and what we would like God to be, the different ways people experience reality, and that other little problem — it's easy to say this book exists because we can see and feel it. And read it. But God? How can we talk about this Being that we can't see?

And that, undoubtedly, is the next question you'll be asked.

"Okay," she'll admit. "If God exists, I guess He's got to exist for everyone. Fine. So are you going to tell me what He's got to do with me, right now?"

So... Our Point Is?

- "Truth is what's real."
- The same thing simply cannot be both true and false. Either a thing is or it isn't, God included.
- Opinions about preferences differ. But it's absurd to say that an opinion that something exists is just as "valid" as an opinion that the same thing doesn't exist.
- Lots of people try to say that all truth is relative or subjective, but no one lives that way. Most of the time when we cop out on truth, we have a reason: We don't want to live by it.
- Don't assume that your friend's position is unassailable. Don't be caught in the trap of thinking your job is just to defend your position. Push her to defend and explain hers, and don't let her hide behind irrational statements.

In Case You've Forgotten...

I thought some definitions might come in handy. Who is God, anyway?

> God is the fullness of Being and of every perfection, without origin and without end. All creatures receive all that they are and have from him, but he alone is his very being, and he is of himself everything that he is.
>
> — *CCC* 213

> God is an Individual, Self-dependent, All-perfect, Unchangeable Being; intelligent, living, personal, and present; almighty, all-seeing, all-remembering . . . who has no origin, who is all sufficient for Himself who created and upholds the universe.
>
> — John Henry Newman, *The Idea of a University*

> "I AM WHO AM."
>
> — Exodus 3:14

> God is love.
>
> — 1 John 4:8

And what about faith?

> Faith is, first of all, personal adherence of man to God. At the same time, and inseparably, it is a *free assent to the whole truth that God has revealed.*
>
> — *CCC* 150

Faith is the realization of what is hoped for and evidence of things not seen.

— Hebrews 11:1

Faith is believing that God believes in you.

— Andre Dubus, "A Father's Story"

So . . . God is the Uncreated One who has loved everything into existence and sustains it.

Faith involves believing that God exists and then saying "yes" to God in a personal way — putting your life in His hands and trusting in His existence, His love, and His purpose for your life.

That's what we're talking about.

CHAPTER 3

I Don't Believe in God Because...

...No One Can Prove
He Exists.

"Prove it!"

"No! You prove it! See! I knew you couldn't do it! You're stupid!"

"You're stupider! You can't prove it either!"

"MOM! She called me stupid!"

Yes, you've grown up now. When someone challenges you to prove that God really exists, we don't replay that particular dialogue.

But yet... aren't you tempted? Wouldn't it be satisfying to just answer this chapter's question with a rapid-fire, "Well, can you prove He doesn't?"

Come to think of it, maybe that's not such a bad idea. Maybe we'll come back to that one later.

But not yet. Let's give the problem what it deserves, and address it head-on.

So you've been told, in all sincerity, "I can't believe in God because no one can prove He exists."

What does that mean? Go ahead and ask. That, by the way, is something we often don't do enough of in our discussions of tough philosophical and theological questions: take the time to ask the person asking questions to elaborate, to explain what they mean. Uptight and ready-to-fire, we probably miss more than we know by not slowing down and listening more.

Most people who make that statement about the unprove-ability of God aren't talking on a really high level. They're not talking about the inadequacy of philosophy to reach conclusions about the infinite God. Well, some are, but they are all pres-ently hunched in little windowless offices in big, ugly concrete university buildings writing impenetrable philosophy papers for journals with a circulation of two. They don't pop up in your lunchroom too often.

No, I'd wager that when a friend declares that God doesn't exist because you can't prove Him, they mean one simple thing:

God isn't accessible to the senses.

You can't see or hear God the same way you can see or hear another person, they'll argue, so how can you know if He exists?

"You can't show me God," your friend announces, "so how can you say He exists?"

Here's what you say:

Does love exist?

Prove it. Just try.

You can't, can you? No one's ever seen or touched love. Sure, you've experienced the effects of love, you think you've felt it, but that's not love itself, in its essence.

> There is nothing beautiful or sweet or great in life that is not mysterious.
>
> — François Rene de Chateaubriand,
> Beauties of the Christian Religion

But even though you can't prove its existence or precisely define it, you still know that love is real, right? Just like hatred or anger or peace of mind? Can you see or touch them? Sometimes we almost feel as if we can — we say that his anger was "almost palpable." But we really can't. Yet who would say there's no such thing as love?

The point is, the world is filled with things that are true and real. Only some of them can ever even come close to being "proven." Another way of saying this is, "Not everything that counts can be counted."

And really, if you think about it, the more important a part of life is, the more difficult it is to talk about precisely, to capture in words or diagram. Not just difficult — impossible.

"Proof" is a concept that's best applied to what's measurable and sensible. We call that the empirical world. Even in that world, the validity of "proof" is much disputed — all it takes is a quick survey of scientific history and current news to determine how hotly debated certain questions of "proof" are in the scientific community. What causes a certain disease? How did the universe start? How did life develop on earth?

If you understood him, it would not be God.
— St. Augustine of Hippo, *Sermons*

So, we can see that "proof" isn't the be-all and end-all of knowledge. Concluding that something exists or happens because of what we observe and reason about it helps us see that some things are true. But lots of very true things can't be definitely proven by observation or the scientific method.

How about God? Your friend is bugging you to prove God exists. He means "show me God." At this point, you're just going to have to say, "I can't," but hope he understands why: that God is one of those very important things in life — like love — that can't be subjected to the tools of science.

Remember who God is? That all-powerful, all-good Being, beyond space and time, who created the universe? Just how in the world can you expect Him to be subject to proof? Proof uses limited human words and just as limited human ideas. If "God" could be adequately captured by words and ideas, if "God" could be pinned down in a neat little proof of three statements, you know what?

He wouldn't be God anymore.

Secondly, God isn't the kind of subject we put under the microscope. If we're serious about God, the One who made us and cares for us, we have to put Him in the same category as the other persons we love and know. You don't get to know a friend by analyzing them, breaking them down into components, and

So . . . Our Point Is?

- When people say they want "proof" that God exists, most of the time they're saying they want empirical evidence — that is, information that can be perceived by the senses.

- Not everything that exists can be proven to exist in that particular, scientific way.

- In fact, some of the most important things in life can't be measured, counted, or proven in the scientific sense.

- God's in that category. Because God is a personal being, we get to know and understand God the same way we get to know people: through listening and understanding.

- If we could prove everything about God in the scientific sense, he wouldn't be God. He'd be more like an amoeba.

then deciding scientifically that they exist and are worthy of your attention.

No. You get to know them. It's a different kind of knowing than scientific inquiry, but just as valid and just as likely to emerge with truth at the other end.

If they're not getting it, or even if you just feel like giving your friend a Great Thought to chew on, ask this question:

What's the "proof" that scientific "proof" is the only way of determining whether something exists? Can you "prove" that point?

Try. And if you go bonkers trying to figure it out, don't blame me. I warned you.

God's Footprints

Got that? Ready to prove that God exists?

Oh. That's right. We said scientific proof isn't the only way of showing that something's true. I think we even said that God is beyond proof. If He weren't, He wouldn't be God. He'd be closer to a centipede than the Creator of the Universe in whom we live and have our being.

Absolutely right. I knew I couldn't sneak this one past you.

I wasn't lying up there. We can't base a relationship of loving faith on what a "proof" can tell us about God because, when you get down to it, He's beyond proof. But neither do we embrace a blind, unthinking, unreasoning faith, either. The decision to love anyone does, indeed, involve a leap of faith, but if it's blind, then it's just stupid. Sure, the person you choose to love could, theoretically, dump you tomorrow, but you base your decision to love on a reasoned (we hope) weighing of the evidence that he probably won't. It's the same with God — our leap of faith is an informed one.

We may not be able to prove that God exists in the same way we can prove what chromosome carries the gene for eye color or how long it takes for light to get here from Alpha Centauri, but we can use our minds to discern evidence in the world around us that points to the existence of God. Like any artist, He's left fingerprints on His creation, for anyone with an open mind to see.

> The whole universe is but the footprint of the divine goodness.
>
> — Dante, *Of Monarchy*

You should take these fingerprints and the conclusions drawn from them seriously. The first of them was formulated by the philosopher Plato more than 2,000 years ago. Plato, by the way, wasn't Christian or Jewish. His ideas about reality, though (for that is what philosophers do, think about reality), have been very influential in helping Jews and Christians think about God. This is a pretty important point to make, by the way:

Who Did That?

It's Saturday morning. A bright, sunny spring morning, too. The only thing bad about it is the cold, cruel truth laid down by your dad that if you want to have a life today at all, the lawn has to be mowed.

Of course, you don't want to do it, but life is life, and you have so many thrilling activities planned, you can't allow a patch of grass to get in your way.

So, out you go to the garage, feed your intimate friend Mr. Lawn Mower, yank on the rope about forty times, and finally, he sputters to life. You're off.

But wait. What's this? In the backyard, peeking through the ankle-high shards of dewy grass, you spy something strange. Are

I Don't Believe in God Because...

they rocks? Are there a lot of them? Wait, they look like they spell something — is there a message here?

Spelled out in the rocks is, "Have fun, sucker!"

Wow.

Now, upon reading these words, what would be the first thought that would come to your mind? Would you murmur to yourself, "My goodness, how odd that somehow during the night, the earth jostled these rocks in a random way that just happened to spell out this helpful message."

I doubt it. You'd probably ask "WHO DID THIS?" It doesn't take you long to figure it out, of course. But alas, your evil sister's already gone. Just wait. Next week's her turn with Mr. Lawn Mower.

Do you see? When we're confronted by an orderly pattern, we don't walk by and say, "What a lovely coincidental arrangement" of paint, words, bricks, or whatever.

The orderly arrangement clearly indicates an arranger.

To put it in the most classical terms: There's no design without a designer. It just doesn't happen. Ever.

Now think about the world around you — orderly seasons, an animal kingdom that unerringly follows instinct generation after generation, a human body of intricate and precise workings, and laws of physics that keep it all from flying right on out into space.

Can anyone who's being intellectually honest really and truly say this came about by chance?

Well, it could have, you might hear in response.

Here comes the time to push.

Don't accept that. Really? It could have? If a camera couldn't happen by chance, how could an eye? Have you ever seen someone throw paint up in the air and watch it come down on the canvas in a realistic landscape? If you blindly dumped random amounts of flour, baking powder, sugar, and chocolate in a bowl and let it sit in the sun, would you end up with brownies?

Quite simply, in reality, does order *ever* emerge from chance?

Well, they might say, grasping for straws, look at the Big Bang. An explosion. A lot of Christians even believe in that theory of the origins of the universe. There's chaos, and here's order. There's an example, right?

> The world is charged with the grandeur of God.
> — Gerard Manley Hopkins, "God's Grandeur"

But, you can remind your friend, even if the theoretical Big Bang really did happen, it obviously wasn't any ordinary explosion. If a factory explodes, do the remnants emerge from the blast artfully and symmetrically arranged, with laws of motion governing their relation to one another? No. Little Bangs result in inert piles of randomly scattered shards of metal and glass. If the Big Bang occurred, it was a unique kind of explosion. Dare we say it was *designed* to result in order in ways that no other explosions do?

Who knows what your friend will think of this, or how he'll respond. He might thoughtfully ponder the implications of an

I Don't Believe in God Because...

obviously designed universe and say he'll get back to you, or he might say something like, "I still don't believe it."

Whatever you say to that, I'd suggest you emphasize a couple of points. Encourage intellectual honesty. Point out that if he can accept the premise that the existence of design necessitates a designer, there's no rational reason for him to say, sure, it applies to paintings and buildings, and everything else he encounters, except the world itself. Keep pushing on this — gently, as always — and you'll probably hear, "I just don't think it is."

Your friend has gone about as far as he can go, so it's usually best to leave it there with a simple question, "Why not? Why not a designer?" You've opened a door, and you've also established belief in a Creator God as a reasonable possibility. No emotions, no subjective feelings to blow off as being fine for you but not for me. Just simple, logical reality.

What's Before the Beginning?

Another way of explaining the existence of God in a reasonable way that anyone, whether a Christian or not, can understand revolves around the concept of cause and effect. It goes something like this:

Nothing causes itself to exist. Nothing creates itself. Everything that exists has a cause. Ultimately, going back and back and back through time, you must, logically speaking, arrive at the point at which there is a First Cause, something that doesn't need to be caused itself but that gets everything else started. A different way to think about God: the First Cause.

You can use the same argument about motion: Nothing moves by itself. All motion is caused by something else — an acorn has fallen on the ground, loosened from its branch by the wind. My foot kicks the acorn from the sidewalk. My will has instructed my foot to do the kicking.

Somewhere, somehow, there has to be something that gets all the motion going, that isn't moved itself. Another way to think about God: the Unmoved Mover.

Now consider existence in itself. The existence of every thing on earth is dependent on something else. The plastic spoon you ate your pudding with at lunch exists because people made machines to shape the plastic into spoons. The plastic exists because petroleum lies under the ground. The petroleum exists because fossils rotted and made a mucky, putrid mess. Fossils exist because the dinosaurs got socked by a comet. The dinosaurs and the comets existed because . . .

Do you see where we're going here?

The existence of every single thing is dependent. Nothing causes itself to exist. Once again, moving backward, we can see that in order for us to even be here, there has to be a being — something — the existence of which isn't dependent on anything else. That something must have existence in and of itself to give. In fact, you could even be led to believe that whatever is back there at the beginning is, in a way, existence or being itself.

There's a lot more we could say about this. People like St. Thomas Aquinas have, if you want to look it up. But we want to keep it simple: All of these arguments help us plug into the basic realities of life that nothing happens without a cause. Nothing moves without being moved. Nothing causes itself to exist. Knowing and accepting all these things, we have to ask, "Okay, then, what was it that caused, that moved, that first existed?"

A voice in the wind I do not know;
A meaning on the face of the high hills
Whose utterance I cannot comprehend.
A something is behind them: that is God.
— George MacDonald, *Within and Without*

Again, it's not "proof" in that scientific sense. It doesn't say anything about God as a being Who loves and cares. But this is what it does: It helps us look at the world and see how that world reveals the logical possibility — some might even say necessity — of a being greater than ourselves, not itself bound by the laws of nature, that got everything we see started. They're clues. Hints. Signs.

They show us that belief in God is a perfectly reasonable answer to the perfectly reasonable question, "How?"

There's More...

There are a lot more arguments that very smart, reasonable, not-crazy people have come up with to point out how God's existence is implicit in the reality around us, if we only look around with open eyes and an open mind. You can have a fantastic old time at the library looking them up, if you like (check out the bibliography at the end for suggestions). But for now, I just want to offer you two more.

Blaise Pascal (1623-1662) was a French mathematician, scientist, and genius-in-general. He was also the founder of probability theory, which is obvious when you consider his very famous statement about God's existence. It's not a proof, or even an argument, but it will give you something to think about anyway. It goes like this:

Every person has a choice:

To accept God's existence or deny it.

If you accept God's existence, and it's true, you've gained everything — eternal life.

If it turns out to be a lie, you haven't lost anything.

If you deny God's existence, and *that* turns out to be a lie — that is, God does (surprise, surprise) exist — you've lost everything, forever.

So where would the smart gambler put her money down?

The last point is one of my favorites. C. S. Lewis points out in *Mere Christianity*, very simply and straightforwardly, that there are no hungers in human existence that cannot be satisfied. If you are thirsty, you can quench your thirst. If you're hungry, you can eat.

> If I find in myself a desire which no experience in this world can satisfy, the most probable explanation is that I was made for another world.
>
> — C. S. Lewis

We're born and live with one more hunger and desire — the desire to exist forever and the desire to be whole and completely at peace. It doesn't seem that any other hunger is impossible to satisfy. Why would that one be?

So . . . Our Point Is?

- You can't "prove" God exists, but that's okay. "Proof" can't tell us everything that's true anyway. There are lots of things we know to be true that could never be proven by empirical or scientific means.

- God's in that category because He's spirit, He's bigger than words and ideas, and He's a person, so it's best to get to know Him as a person, not an idea or theory.

- But God does leave evidence of His existence in His creation. The universe is very carefully designed. We know that if everything exists or moves, there must be a cause to that existence and motion. The existence of standards and even meaning itself indicates the existence of One who gives meaning, and thus IS the highest standard.

- There's no human hunger or desire that can't be satisfied. We all yearn for wholeness and eternal life . . . why would that be the only human hunger that exists just to be frustrated?

- And what about this: Why, you might ask, is there *something* instead of *nothing*, anyway?

CHAPTER 4

I Don't Believe in God Because...

...Science Shows That the Universe Exists Without a God.

"GREAT," YOUR FRIEND says. "Nice ideas, and they almost make sense, all that stuff about design and a designer and everything."

Gee, thanks.

"But you know, there's one big problem here. You say that a God made us. Created the universe — everything."

Yup. She finally gets the idea. I rock.

"Then why doesn't science talk about God? Scientific theories about the universe and life and everything don't bring God into it. The Big Bang and evolution and all that — they work fine without God. There's no need for God and no room for him either. I think those guys know what they're talking about, don't you?"

Drat. Can I go home now? Please?

So, is that true? Does modern scientific knowledge make God irrelevant?

You'd think so, from the way you've been taught. After all, science teachers treat these subjects in a thoroughly secular framework, droning on about black holes and that delicious primordial soup. Who needs God?

The first thing to do when you're faced with this question is be reasonable. Always, always be reasonable and encourage all you meet to embrace the same, admittedly novel attitude.

We study all kinds of subjects that we may know God has a hand in. After all, if we're people of faith, we believe God's hand is in everything, right? But just because we believe that doesn't mean we're constantly bringing God into our studies and discussions in an explicit way.

It's obvious that Shakespeare and Mozart were both gifted with amazing talents by God. We know this, but what we say in our discussions and analysis of the work they produced assumes God's mysterious role and concentrates on the words and notes before us.

There's a time and a place for everything. There's a time to study the antislavery movement as a historical event, and there's another time to reflect on its spiritual dimensions, as one more step in humanity's gradual understanding of God's call for us to treat each other as brothers and sisters, equal in His eyes.

It's the same with science. Scientists are dedicated to uncovering the mechanics, the cause and effect behind the universe as it's worked out through physical laws and chemical reactions. Even if you believe that God's involved in that process, His involvement isn't anything you can harness or use for humanity's benefit. So, excuse us if we're not continually hauling God into our scientific discussions. After all, up until the present day, the vast majority of scientists throughout history have also been believers in God. Even today, surveys indicate that around 40 percent of scientists believe in God, including some Nobel Prize winners and other important people. They didn't — and don't — see overwhelming obstacles in integrating what they've learned about life as it is with their faith that God's at the heart of it. We don't, either.

Your next hurdle, I will guarantee, will be your friend's assumption that religion and science are mortal enemies. It's quite likely that she's working out of some mythic, stereotypical mental image of history in which religious people — sporting hateful scowls and big, fat blinders — have been engaged in hundreds of years of battle with scores of noble, truth-telling, and always oppressed scientists. You hear a lot of that these days.

The truth — I mean the cold, hard, unbiased truth — is that for the vast majority of Christian history, scientific and religious views have not been at odds. Historians of science even suggest that the phenomenal progress of scientific knowledge in Europe from the fifteenth through the nineteenth centuries (something that didn't happen anywhere else in the world at the same level) may be due to that culture's deeply Christian worldview, which saw scientific exploration as a way of honoring God and His creation.

The list of scientists who were also devout Christians is a long one. Here are a few — any familiar names?

Nicolaus Copernicus, who formulated the theory that the earth revolved around the sun, worked as an administrator in the Catholic Church in his native Poland.

> How could anyone observe the right order with which God governs the universe without feeling himself inclined... to the practice of all virtues, and to the beholding of the Creator Himself, the source of all goodness, in all things and before all things?
>
> — Nicolaus Copernicus, Preface, *De Revolutionibus*

Johann Kepler, who discovered the planets' elliptical motion and formulated what you've probably studied as Kepler's Laws of Planetary Motion, said that scientists, above all, should be "thoughtful, not of the glory of our minds, but rather, above all else, of the glory of God."

Blaise Pascal, one of the great early mathematicians (you can lay the blame for calculus partly on his shoulders) was a deeply

devout Catholic who left a still-popular book of spiritual reflections called the *Pensées*.

Isaac Newton, who takes the rest of the blame for calculus, discovered the law of gravity and the three laws of motion, also wrote books reflecting his strong faith in Christ.

Gregor Mendel, the father of genetics, the guy who grew all of those peas in a monastery garden? He was an Augustinian monk.

And here's one that you probably don't know: Georges Lemaitre, who worked out the theory of the Big Bang origins of the universe in the 1920s, was a Catholic priest.

Oh, yes. If science and religion are so diametrically opposed, why is one of the oldest astronomical institutes in the world run by the Vatican — you know — the central authority in the Roman Catholic Church?

It's true. Going back to the eighteenth century, the Vatican has funded and operated a series of astronomical observatories.

Since the mid-twentieth century, the central location has been at Castel Gandolfo outside of Rome, which also happens to be the pope's summer residence.

Yeah, that's it. Believers cower in fear before the specter of scientific exploration and discovery. A priest figured out the Big Bang, a monk discovered genetics, and the pope's got a huge telescope at his summerhouse. Please. Can we get over the stereotypes and talk about reality now?

"Everyone knows that scientific discoveries have taught us that there's no room or need for God in the universe."

Really? Like what? Tell me more!

"Like the Big Bang, the beginning of the universe. We studied it in science class, remember? There's no God in that theory. Evolution, too. That really put the nail in the coffin, didn't it? Life on earth happened and develops because of natural selection and mutation. No God there, either."

But is what we learned the truth, the whole truth, and nothing but the truth about this stuff?

Meaningful, thoughtful silence.

Well, is it?

It is, indeed, what you've been taught: There's no room for God in the universe or in the origins of life because, after all, armies of friendly scientists have proven that everything in the universe, from its explosive beginning to the development of the horsefly, is explainable by purely natural causes that leave no room for God.

I cannot say this strongly enough:

This is not true.

You might be surprised to learn that God is actually a pretty hot topic in some scientific discussions these days. There are more unanswered questions in physics, cosmology, and evolution than ever, and the puzzles scientists are finding where they once thought they'd discover natural explanations, just open up the possibility that there really is more on earth — and in heaven — than we really know.

Who Detonated the Big Bang?

As I mentioned before, the groundwork for the Big Bang Theory was laid by a Belgian Catholic priest. His math was confirmed by evidence a few years later by astronomer Edwin Hubble, whose observations of "red shift" (is it all coming back to you now?) led to the conclusion that — gasp! — the universe was expanding, which meant it had to have a beginning to expand from. It's sort of like that First Cause theory in the last chapter, right? Aristotle and Aquinas didn't have telescopes, but they just might have been on to something, anyway.

Back to the Big Bang. Believe it or not, quite a few scientists hated this theory when it was first developed. These hostile scientists also happened to be atheists. They were appalled by the consequences of suggesting that the universe had a beginning. After all, if there was a beginning, then the question arises... what was there to explode, and where did it come from? Hmmmm?

So, interestingly enough, the Big Bang theory that most of us take for granted was originally opposed by atheists because it implied the existence of God.

Now that's an interesting possibility, isn't it?

"Suspiciously Suited for Life"

Did you know...

That if the forces binding atoms were five percent weaker than they are, hydrogen would be the only stable element in the universe, and life wouldn't exist?

I Don't Believe in God Because...

That if those same forces were two percent weaker, hydrogen would not be stable and no hydrogen-containing compounds could form — you know, like water?

Put it this way:

> Even the most minor tinkering with the value of the funda-
> mental forces of physics — gravity, electromagnetism, the
> nuclear strong force, or the nuclear weak force — would
> have resulted in an unrecognizable universe.[1]

There's a whole discussion going on right now about these matters, under the heading of the "Anthropic Theory."

All the seemingly arbitrary and unrelated constants in physics have one strange thing in common — these are precisely the values you need if you want to have a universe capable of producing life. The question your friend needs to confront with openness and honesty is this: Is such specific fine-tuning, this arrangement of the universe according to laws and conditions so suspiciously suited for life really just the product of forces without purpose or direction?

Does fine-tuning ever happen by accident?

> The existence of a being endowed with intelligence and
> wisdom is a necessary inference from a study of celestial
> mechanics.
>
> — Isaac Newton, *Principia*

Evolving

Ah, yes. Evolution. Finally — we're here.

This is *supposed* to be it. This is supposed to be the point when you and your atheist friend finally part ways because, of

---

[1] Patrick Glynn, *God: the Evidence* (Prima Publishing, 1999), p. 29.

course, the scientific theory of evolution proves that God doesn't exist.

Funny thing, though. When you look up, say, "evolution" and "popes," or "evolution" and "Catholic Church," what do you find?

You'll find something surprising. You'll find that the Catholic Church has *never* condemned the scientific theory of evolution or declared that Catholics should run away when they hear the word.

Not at all.

"Evolution" as a theory has many different components, but fundamental to the theory are the ideas that all life on earth descends from a common origin, and that individual forms of life have developed — evolved — as adaptations to their environments.

In 1950, Pope Pius XII indicated that evolution — a theory then about a century old, as Darwin articulated it — was not necessarily in conflict with Christian beliefs about human origins and purpose.

Not necessarily.

For, of course, it could be. And there are certain ways of thinking about evolution and applying it to human life that do stand in opposition to the truths God has revealed to us: when evolutionary theory leads people to conclude that God is unnecessary, or that human beings have no free will, or that life has no purpose, or (as was common in the nineteenth and early twentieth centuries) that certain races are inferior to others because they haven't "evolved" as much — well, that's a problem.

And to be sure, there are certainly plenty of scientists out there who do, indeed, see evolutionary theory as an argument against God. We have to be honest about that.

But, as Pope Pius XII and other popes (not to mention *lots* of Christian thinkers) have pointed out since, there isn't an intrinsic conflict between the idea that God is the author of life and that God used the mechanism of evolution to create that life.

So as you talk about evolution to your friend, just be sure to remember the following points:

- Genesis — the first book of the Bible — reveals to us certain truths about the *why* we are here as well as truths about our nature: we're good, we're made in God's image, we have a purpose, and sin happens when we violate God's will for us. It's all very true, but it's not necessarily *scientific* truth.

- Evolutionary theory doesn't present an automatic, intrinsic challenge to God's existence or work in the world. The Catholic Church has never taught that.

Evolutionary theory, though, is a *theory* and has changed and, well . . . evolved over the decades itself. It is not (pardon the pun) Gospel. It can be abused and misused, even in ways that hurt people.

As a side note, this might be a good time to toss out some cautions about that whole "science" thing, especially if your friend seems to have latched onto it as, well, another religion.

That happens, you know. "Science" is the answer to everything. If we can't "prove" something or if there's not enough "evidence," well, too bad. It must not be real. And if it's in a scientific journal or book and if enough "scientists" believe it . . . it must be true, as they articulate it . . . right now.

Well, here's the thing about that mindset.

It really does take faith to believe it.

Every step in knowledge — even scientific knowledge — begins with an act of faith.

It begins with the belief that my brain can perceive what my senses tell me is here and make sense of it, and that the result of all that is . . . reality. It begins with faith in the existence of Truth.

Maybe there isn't such a huge divide between faith and reason after all.

Maybe they need each other.

Maybe they are actually ways of seeing different parts of life, and one needs the other. Most of this book has been about showing how we can be comfortable with the reasonableness of faith. This part is about showing how even the most coldly reasoned, rational scientific theory begins with a step of faith.

So in response to your friend's questions, just make those points over and over. Invite him to look at the evidence with an open mind. Admit that this evidence doesn't "prove" God — we've been over how God's not provable, anyway. Shrug your shoulders and admit that, of course, the evidence pointing to an Intelligent Designer in charge of existence doesn't tell us anything about a personal God who loves and saves us. We learn about all that in other ways.

Just ask, and push your friend gently: Given an honest look at the evidence — does belief in God really still seem so crazy, irrational, or pathetically primitive, after all?

An atheist is a man who believes himself an accident.

— Francis Thompson, *Paganism, Old and New*

The argument that nature's design implies a designer is thousands of years old. Some people thought that modern physics and evolutionary theory killed it.

What a surprise. It didn't.

So . . . Our Point Is?

- Science and religion aren't at odds. They're different ways of exploring different aspects of the same reality: life.

- Modern science was born out of a Judeo-Christian culture and, for the most part, from the minds of devout Christians, Jews, and Muslims.

- Contemporary science hasn't disproved God; in fact, as we know more about life, the evidence points more strongly to God, as the Intelligent Designer of all that is, than it ever did.

- Modern theories of cosmology (the origins of the universe) reveal that the universe's cohesiveness, order, and congeniality to life is the result of physical and chemical relations so precisely balanced that if they were off even slightly, life would not be possible.

- The Catholic Church does not teach that evolution is wrong. Catholics are free to believe in evolutionary theory or not. The Church *does* teach that any scientific theory of the origins of life we believe must enable us to believe in God as the source of life and human beings uniquely created in God's image.

- All knowledge, even scientific knowledge, involves a bit of faith.

I Don't Believe in God Because...

CHAPTER 5

I Don't Believe in God Because...

...People Could Have Just Made the Stuff in the Bible UP.

... YOU COULD BE the mutant child of space aliens.

... Dinosaurs could be flourishing in a vast underground holding pen in the middle of the Sahara Desert.

... Consuming mass quantities of Buffalo wings could prevent the flu.

... And yes, "they" could have just made up everything that's in the Bible.

But did they?

I can't tell you how many times I've heard that statement at the top of the page, flung out casually at the end of a class discussion. What makes it funny (besides the fact that it's pretty dumb) is that whoever says it always seems to think they have formed nothing less than the most brilliant observation ever to fall from human lips. It's as if their speculation is so cunning and clever that it has the power to just shut everyone up and close the door on any reasoned discussion of Christian claims about God.

Because, you know, they could have made everything up.

Like over the past few thousand years, no one had ever thought of testing the Bible for historical accuracy.

Like none of the hundreds of millions of Christians who've walked the earth and contemplated their faith had ever wondered if any of it were historically verifiable and taken the time to check it out before they decided it was true.

> A denial of God is practically always the result of shutting one eye. It may be for this reason that God gave us two.
>
> — C. A. Coulson, *Science and Christian Belief*

Yeah, right. Thanks, genius. We never thought of that. What would we do without you?

If I seem a little harsh here, well, I am. Some arguments against the possibilities of God's existence have some intellectual weight and complexity to them. This one doesn't, which makes it all the more frustrating because you hear it so often. Try not to laugh when you do. Instead, just invite your friend to take a calm, reasoned walk through reality with you. It won't take long. Here goes:

As I pointed out at the beginning of this chapter, lots and lots of things "could have" happened. That's the pleasure of creating and reading fiction, in fact — to give our imaginations free rein in the land of the "could haves."

But they didn't. Some things happened and other things didn't. How do you know the difference in general, and then, how do you apply that to the Bible?

Let's apply it to something else first. Did Julius Caesar exist? Is there any way to know for sure, or are we forever lost in a sea of agnosticism about the existence and achievements of the guy?

Of course, there are ways of establishing whether Julius Caesar existed and what he did in his time on this earth. It's called history.

Historians start with evidence, any kind they can get their hands on. They use physical evidence, from what's left of ancient buildings to weapons, shards of pottery, art, and gravesites. They study ancient documents of every kind, from literature to government records. They study migration and climate patterns. They examine the earth close up and from the sky to figure out where ancient people lived, why they moved, and what caused their civilizations to flourish and decline. This business of figuring out what happened in the past is not a crapshoot. It's an established, ancient discipline with high standards of study and reasoning.

And here's the big news: Historians have given just as much energy to the study of the events of Biblical times — from the origins of the Hebrew people in the sands of the Iraqi desert to the apostle John's exile on the island of Patmos 2,500 years later — as they have to any other subject in the past. Probably more. And you know what? There's not one scholar of any discipline or any religious sensibility anywhere on the planet Earth who would say the Bible was simply "made up."

To put it bluntly, then, saying that the content of the Bible could have been just fabricated is nothing but ignorant.

Secular historians who study the ancient Near East use the Old and New Testament as sources, and they consistently find that it is generally quite reliable in what it relates about ancient Israelite culture and history, as well as what hints it gives us about other cultures of the time.

Archaeologists have discovered inscriptions mentioning the "House of David," Pilate, Caiaphas, and other Biblical figures. They've discovered that the Philistines were indeed, as the Old Testament claims, expert metal workers. Historians have concluded that the amount of money quoted by the author of Genesis as what Joseph's brothers got for selling him to slavery was indeed what the going slave rate was during the time the events in the story were supposed to have taken place. In 1968, the remains of a crucified man were discovered outside of Jerusalem. The wounds they found — from the nails through the ankles and broken shinbones — corroborate the Gospel's accounts of what was done to Jesus on the cross.

Further, when you read the Bible closely (something your friend should definitely be invited to do) and use common sense, you see signs all over the place that the people who wrote and gathered the materials in the Bible were very serious about what they were doing, knew what they were doing, and had no intentions of deceiving anyone.

One of the most powerful pieces of evidence for this is the fact that the great figures of the Bible are presented truthfully, warts and all. Almost every one of them, from Abraham to Moses and beyond, questions and argues with God. The first king of Israel, Saul, committed suicide. The next monarch, David, got another man's wife pregnant and then had the husband killed. If you're going to make up stories about your religion, it's highly unlikely that you'd create such strange, sad stories, heavy with tragedy and even ambiguity, at the heart of it.

Look at it this way. Say you had started a religion, and to get other people to join, you've decided to make up some stories about your amazing origins. First, going back to the Old Testament again, would you have your great and glorious people descended from a bunch of slaves? Consider Christianity's founder and his assistants. If you were making up stories about them, would you have the assistants be a bunch of unfailingly dense, squabbling guys who could never quite grasp the point of what their leader was talking about and often fell way short in their levels of faith? Would you have the head of those assistants betray the founder at a crucial moment? Would you have the major, amazing miracle of your founder's life — his resurrection from the dead — be discovered by women, an entire segment of the population whose testimony would never, ever have been accepted as valid in the courts of their time?

No. When people make up stories about figures they want others to see as heroes, they make those heroes superhuman and idealized — they don't have them weep, get angry, mourn over friends, and die the deaths of criminals. Anyone who's ever even taken an hour to read over ancient mythology can tell a clear difference between those idealized, moralistic fables and the very real human world of struggling faith and gradual understanding we see in the Jewish and Christian Scriptures.

Once we've gotten over the absurd suggestion that the Bible's a work with no historical usefulness, we have to get at another dimension of the question.

It's quite likely that a part of your friend's confusion about the truthfulness of the Bible is rooted in a misunderstanding about exactly what the Bible is. He might conclude that since many Catholics as well as Protestants and Jews don't, for example, take the story of Adam and Eve as literal, historical truth, this means that the entire Bible should be read in the same way.

Why, your friend wants to know, should I take the Bible seriously as a place to find truth about God (or anything) when there are parts of it you, Ms. Believer, don't even think are "true"? Isn't the whole enterprise suspect, then?

What you have to do here is backtrack and discuss some simple facts about truth, literature, God, and not being a nitwit when you read.

First, point out that the Bible isn't really one book. It's seventy-three different books collected in a single volume. It's like a little library there, between two covers, and like any library, it contains books of different types and styles. It contains poetry, history, civic records, a couple of short stories, prophecy, letters, and a unique form of biographical writing called Gospels.

Just as you would, quite frankly, be an idiot for walking into the school library and reading a volume of Emily Dickinson's poetry with the same expectations you bring to a history of the

French Revolution, you can't read Psalms the exact same way you read the Book of Chronicles. Job demands something different of the reader than Exodus does.

Certainly, the reader is looking in all of the books of the Bible for God's revealed word, which is true. That's consistent, no matter where your Bible falls open. But what changes is what God uses to express that truth.

Remember what truth is? Truth is what's real, right? So what we find in the Bible is a collection of books that express the Truth that God has revealed to us about Himself and us — who He is, His relationship with us, and who we are.

Now think about how you express your ideas. Do you simply write them out in plain sentences of literal words? You do? Oh. Remind me not to read *your* books, then.

No, plain, factual, literal words just aren't enough to express thought, are they? It's why we create paintings, sculptures, and symphonies. It's why we write poems, essays, and novels. It's why we dance.

Human beings don't just speak literally all the time. Think how boring it would be if we did. We fill our language with metaphors and similes. We create images with meter and rhyme in poetry. We analyze the doings of historical figures and we are swept up in the lives of imaginary ones. We say it's raining cats and dogs, when it would be just as "factual" to say it's raining hard. We read *Johnny Tremain,* when we could just as well read a straight history of the Revolutionary War.

Put it this way: In telling the truth about life, human beings use every tool at their disposal — historical memory and reporting, scientific analysis, and even imaginations.

God knows this, and in the Bible, we see God doing the very same thing: using various literary forms and genres and types of writers to get His message across.

Your friend needs to understand this: *truth is broader than fact.* It's a point related to the one we made a few pages ago — not everything that counts can be counted, right? All facts are true, but not all truth is expressed in literal, factual terms. There are some parts of the Bible that are not factual, and the people who committed those stories to paper weren't terribly concerned with that question, either. They were just fine with the whole concept of expressing truth in non-factual literary forms. They understood that what was most important, for example, about the early stories in Genesis, is what they're telling us about the nature of creation and how we've screwed up the great gift of life and intimacy God's given us. Perhaps those stories are rooted in ancient memories of real events. Who knows? But we read them as vitally true expressions of what God wants to tell us about who we are.

There is, however, quite a bit of history in the Bible, and as I've previously pointed out, modern scholars of every religion and specialty believe most of the historical material in the Bible is trustworthy. This is important, because Judaism and Christianity are decidedly historical religions. Our faith is rooted in the ways we believe God enters human history, reveals Himself to us, and reaches out to us, from Creation to ancient Israel to Jesus himself. The question, then, isn't "Did Jesus exist?" There's no question He existed, and the apostles and writers of the Gospel had no motivation for making up what they said about Him. The single remaining question is what's our response to it all — to the Scriptures as a whole, and Jesus in particular?

So what you say is simple. If someone announces that they're not going to take your faith seriously because the stuff in the Bible could have been just made up out of the blue, push them on it. Ask them to share their great knowledge of biblical history with you and point out how that's so. Ask them to explain what would motivate communities of believers to fabricate stories, especially stories that frequently portray their founding fathers and mothers in flawed, imperfect ways. Ask her when the last time she seriously read the Bible was and how closely she's studied it. I'll wager she hasn't read it at all, much less studied it. Tell her she can do better than that, and invite her to try.

So . . . Our Point Is?

- First you challenge. What's the basis of saying that? What authority has your friend read that asserts that the Bible's "all made up"? What studies from ancient history and archaeology is she basing this sweeping condemnation on?

- Once she's admitted the truth, which can be nothing but, "none," try to be more positive.

- Talk about how the historical material in the Bible is generally reliable. Talk about what the Bible actually says about Jewish and Christian history and how honest it is about the failings present in the past. Liars don't make up lies that present themselves unflatteringly.

- Invite her to read the Bible herself with an open mind — starting with a Gospel — to see if it strikes her as generally authentic or not, and what she has to say about the Jesus whose story it is.

CHAPTER 6

I Don't Believe in God Because...

...It's So Difficult to Find Him.

SHOULDN'T IT BE easier?

After all, we're talking about God here, the God we describe as the omnipotent, omniscient creator of the universe. Omnipresent, too — that means everywhere. Given all of that, shouldn't it be as easy to find God as it is to figure out that you're in the middle of the ocean when you're surrounded by saltwater, waves, and strings of seaweed?

Thinking about it that way — on its simplest level — sure, it should be easier. But (as you might expect) we're not satisfied with simple here. Given the opportunity, we can't avoid the chance to engage in Deep Thoughts and, even better, incredibly Apt Analogies.

Have your friend think about this question first: Just because we're in the presence of something, does that mean we automatically recognize it for what it is?

You're at a friend's house. His mom presents you with her favorite dish for dinner. You're a polite fellow, so you dig in. It tastes pretty good, and you're considering asking for seconds when the mom reads your mind and asks, "So I see you're enjoying my secret prize-winning recipe for pig lips braised in prune juice, Chip! Do you want some more?"

Now we'll see how polite you really are.

Do you see? You were on pretty intimate terms with those pig lips, but you had no idea as to their true identity. You didn't have enough information — like what pig lips in prune juice would taste like — to identify it.

Have you ever been with a group of people when afterwards, someone asked, "Did you notice how upset Brittany was?" — and you had no idea Brittany was even mildly depressed, much less emotionally devastated, that her GPA had dropped under 4.4? I wouldn't be surprised if you've been on the other side, too, surrounded by people who just don't understand or even notice your emotions.

Finally, try this. Imagine that you have to tell someone else who you are. You have to cover every external detail and every facet of your personality. And at the end, you have to write a paragraph that defines you in all of your glorious, unique, incomparable essence.

Can you do it? Why not, for heaven's sake? You're present to yourself constantly. You've lived with yourself for years, day and night. You've been witness to your own most intimate thoughts. If anyone should be able to describe you it should be you, right? Why is it so hard?

Let that sink in for a bit. If we can't precisely define the selves we live with in physical, emotional, psychological, and spiritual intimacy, how can we expect to be able to define God?

What we're talking about here is *knowing*. Philosophers call it "epistemology." There are two basic kinds of knowing: one kind is apprehending and understanding *about* something or someone and the other kind is *being in relation* with another. You can know *about* someone, but that doesn't mean you *know* them. You can even be in relation with someone and not know much about the facts of their lives.

Both kinds of knowing seem as if they should be simple and stress-free. After all, if you've got your senses and your brain, shouldn't information and knowledge about things as they are just kind of drift inside you and stick?

Well, that's not the way it works, and after years of school-work and trying to understand your parents, you've figured this out, haven't you? Neither kind of knowing comes easily, even if we're talking about something as apparently simple as knowing about the structure of a cell or simply knowing another person.

Sure, we can study and even memorize the chart of the cell's internal structure that's staring at us from our biology book, but does that chart give us everything that's knowable about the cell? No. Microbiologists are continually discovering new aspects of cell life and mechanics, and science is filled with examples of "sure" scientific knowledge upended by the next Galileo or Einstein.

So it's not easy to know about the objects that are literally under our noses. It's not easy to know other people, even ourselves.

> **If I cannot completely know even a daisy, still less can I completely know God.**
> — Baron von Hugel, *Letters to a Niece*

Then, why does the fact that God can be difficult to find and understand surprise us? If we can't describe the "ourselves" we can touch, feel, and are present to twenty-four hours a day precisely and completely, if we can't get to the bottom of who we really are, how can we expect God to be what we're not? How could God be God if we could put Him in boxes made of words and diagrams, then present Him, neatly packaged and instantly accessible, to each person at birth?

So you should see by now that the argument that God can't exist because He can be difficult to "find" doesn't work. You may be hard to understand and impossible to know completely. But you exist. Don't you?

It's important to point out other reasons why knowing God is difficult. In telling each other about God, we're limited because the words we use are limited. If you've ever tried to express the depth of what you feel about another person or a particular moment, you know how true this is. Words aren't ever enough, it seems. In talking about God, we understand this usefulness, yet limitations of words.

> Ever since the days of Adam, man has been hiding from God and saying, "God is hard to find."
> — Bishop Fulton Sheen, *Peace of Soul*

We also have problems finding God because of the shadows that affect our perception. Back in the first chapter, we talked about how people's past experiences shape their opinions about God. None of us sees clearly, as St. Paul says. Our perceptions of all of reality — not just God — are biased by our experiences, our prejudices, our ignorance, and our expectations.

Say you're taking Algebra II. You've never liked math, ever. You'd rather be reading Emily Dickinson or painting waterfalls any day before you do a math problem. Besides that, your Algebra I teacher really reeked. Not literally, but in terms of teaching ability. You didn't really learn a thing. Your present teacher promises to be almost as bad.

So, here you are. You have no background, you're negative about the subject, and the person who's trying to teach you is incompetent. How much algebra are you going to learn this year?

Does that mean algebra doesn't exist?

Ask your friend to consider her own rejection of God, and see if she has anything in common with that poor, hapless algebra student.

Does she have much background in what Christianity actually and really teaches about God?

Did she have good "teachers" who've known what they were talking about and lived it?

Does she have an open mind, unbiased about any possibility of God being real?

If she's answering "no" to those questions, you can tell her the simple truth. Of course, she's going to reject God. Her mind is narrow and closed. You can't learn about anything that way.

This is a pretty simple point to make, but very important. You're not offering any great, complex proofs or demonstrations. You're just pointing out how wrong it is to presume that because there are mysteries at the core of life that make things difficult to describe, challenging to know, and impossible to define, that those things don't exist. We wouldn't say that about any other aspect of existence — that because you're indefinable and sort of a pain to get to know, you don't exist. Why do we say it of God?

So . . . Our Point Is?

- There are two kinds of "knowing": knowing in a personal way, and knowing about.

- Both kinds of knowing are difficult. Why?

- There is a mystery at the heart of everything that exists that makes it impossible to completely and precisely define.

- In our attempts to know or know about, we're limited by our perceptions, the inadequacies of the words we use, our biases, and our ignorance.

- Those limitations are challenges that apply to knowing, and knowing about, everything. God's not exempt. But all of those things that are difficult to know about, and that can never be known completely, exist nonetheless. God can, too.

CHAPTER 7

I Don't Believe in God Because...

...People Have So Many Different Ideas About Him.

This might be a tough one.

Because your friend is absolutely right. People do have wildly different ideas about God.

Throughout history, human beings have never failed to sense a "more" to human life. It's right up there with the instinct to survive and reproduce — every culture, past and present, leaves evidence of the attention paid to that "more." They've left talismans, totems, and sacrificial altars still stained with blood. They've left cathedrals and great golden statues of Buddha. Despite the claims that we presently live in a secular age, it's a plain fact that we still acknowledge and try to connect with the "more" — from Christian youth groups to ancient monasteries still in use, we know it's there. We still seek and we still hunger to name and know the "more."

And you can't deny that in trying to name this "more," people have come up with radically different ideas to describe it. Well, you could, but you'd look really stupid:

- Animists in ancient and indigenous cultures believe that the "more" resides in the earth and its creatures. A lot of modern New Age beliefs pick up on this strain of thinking.

- Polytheists have believed that many gods with different powers are in control of various aspects of life. Popular

Hinduism is the one remaining world religion that's still polytheistic in its outlook.

- Monists believe that the "more" is all of reality, and that there's really no such thing as individual existence — it's an illusion. Hindus believe this, too, and Buddha taught it in a radical way.

- Monotheists believe that there's one God, responsible for creation, accessible to it, but still at root separate from it. Muslims, Jews, and Christians are monotheists. But even among us monotheists, there are differences, right? Christians believe that Jesus is God, and that God is Trinity — three persons in one God. Jews and Muslims don't believe that, of course.

At this point, does this whole situation bring to mind the rough draft of your last English paper, a huge mess with lots of ideas, contradictions, and no center? We've reached an interesting point here — there are plenty of good reasons to believe that God exists, we accept that it could be challenging to learn about Him, but just what are we going to make of the diversity of views about what, exactly, is true about God?

> Contradiction is no more an indication of falsehood than lack of it is an indication of truth.
>
> — Blaise Pascal, *Pensées*

To start, we need to go back one more time to the issue of knowledge.

Consider a topic that's not quite as big as God, but still controversial. If you've studied your American history, you know that historians have different theories about the causes of the Civil War. You might even have had to write a paper about those different ideas. Why, you wonder, can't they just come to an agreement about what got this terrible event underway?

I Don't Believe in God Because...

Two basic reasons: First, different historians have various intellectual and ideological biases that affect how they see their work. Second, not any one of them, or even all of them together, have complete access to and understanding of the entire experience of the origins of the Civil War, which, if you want to get down to it, goes way back before 1861 — if you want to get cosmic about it, even further back to the first sin committed by the first person, anyway.

So we're back again to the constraints of human knowledge: the limitations of the human mind and the plain fact that we never have complete information about anything.

But, does that mean there wasn't a cause to the Civil War?

No. Just because we can't fully grasp or describe it doesn't mean there isn't a cause, and by cause I don't mean a single event. I mean a set of occurrences and influences that brought that particular event to birth. We can't ever give a complete accounting of it, but there was indeed a cause — or, more realistically, a number of causes.

Let's take a different kind of example. Think of someone in your family — a parent, sibling, or grandparent. Maybe Cousin Effie. Does everyone else in the family see Effie in exactly the same way? Would she be described in the exact same terms by everyone who knows her? No, she wouldn't. Why? Same reason. Every one of you has a different experience of her. One-half appreciates her undying interest in everyone's private lives as an expression of her deep love and concern, and everyone else wishes she'd just mind her own business.

But, does that mean there's no Cousin Effie? If we all have different experiences and descriptions of who she is, that's not her fault. It's ours. She exists. Our individual limits make it impossible to see her as she is (Remember the last chapter?) and they also make it inevitable that we'll each see her differently.

Now move on back to God. Yes, there are a multitude of different views of God. But that doesn't mean there's no truth at the heart of our various limited perceptions. Our cultures, our sins, our measly brains and hearts affect what we'll be able to see and say about God.

So, we're limited in what we can know and say, but that doesn't automatically mean the thing we're trying to talk about doesn't exist.

But does it make the *opposite* true? Does it mean that anything we say about God is true? If God is really amazingly beyond our perceptions and definitions, does that mean any definition is okay?

They'll want it to be; believe me, they will. Why? Because it's easy, and it postpones the unpleasant necessity of thinking logically about what they're saying. But don't let them.

Just because there are lots of different opinions about the origins of the Civil War, that doesn't mean we can say it was caused by the Muslim invasion of the Holy Land. You think Cousin Effie's a gem, I think she's a pain — but no one can say she's a Tibetan monk.

> **It is the error of cowards to mistake a difficulty for an impossibility.**
> — Jacques Maritain, *Introduction to Philosophy*

So it goes with God. God may be infinite and God may be spirit. But that doesn't mean God is anything we decide He is.

First of all, it's not logical. You're either eating pizza or you're not. You can't be both at the same time. God simply cannot be both the One who told ancient Aztecs to murder thousands upon thousands of children in sacrifice and the One who says, "Thou shalt not kill." The One who shapes life cannot be both ultimately the extinction of what just *seems* to be — as Buddhists believe — *and at the same time* the loving Cause of being who creates individual, unique immortal souls to live on earth and then dwell with Him forever.

God can be a lot, but He can't contradict Himself.

So what do we do now? Despair? How in the world can we know anything about God?

Pause. Take a deep breath. Look around. Just keep thinking — *other people have thought about this, too. I'm not the only one.*

But there's something else. We've reached an interesting point here. It's called the end of the line. We may have concluded that the existence of different ideas about God doesn't mean that every notion people hold about God is true. But what is true, beyond what those fingerprints a few chapters back tell us?

Not much. There's nothing wrong with admitting it, either. Philosophy and ideas have brought us a long way from total denial of God. We've seen that there's a lot we can know about God from reason and nature. We can figure out that God, as First Cause and Prime Mover and all of that, exists. We can see that while it's hard to know Him, He's knowable. We can see that God is that "more" for which every human being who's ever lived yearns.

But that's about it.

You are perfectly free to admit that human reason — which, while able to know about God, is so clouded by smallness, weakness, and sin — can take us no farther.

So what's next?

He has a name.

Jesus.

Who knows how far your friend has come with you by this time? If she's been open-minded and you've been reasonably coherent, she might actually be intellectually open to the fact that the existence of God is not only possible, but necessary — that she couldn't and wouldn't be here if God wasn't, either. But she's frustrated, and understandably so, by her own limitations of understanding and that of every other person who's tried to think about these questions.

What next?

Gently, ever so mildly, mention Jesus.

Here's the deal, in its simplest terms. Take it or leave it, you can say.

Jesus lived. No one doubts that. He did amazing things and affected people deeply. He talked about God, God's love and forgiveness, and even hinted that He had a special, unique relationship with God. He was executed, and three days later, His followers and friends saw Him alive again.

This resurrection thing could take up a whole other book, of course, and it might seem a little off track, but it's really important to talk about it here.

Lots of people have tried to come up with arguments against Jesus' resurrection, but every one of them falls flat in the face of the historical record, common sense, and this very, very important consequence:

After the apostles saw Jesus risen, and after Pentecost, every one of them gave his life to spreading the Good News that Jesus was the Messiah, the Savior promised by God. His actions were God's actions on earth. He was killed, but He rose from the dead.

Every one of the apostles spent the rest of his life talking about this. They left everything, sacrificed all they had known, and most died with the name of Jesus on their lips.

People just don't do this for a lie.

Sure, people die for untruths, things they've been taught and never had a chance to evaluate for themselves. But they don't

get crucified and burned for a lie about a supposedly direct experience. What possible motivation would the apostles have for doing such a thing? There wasn't any money, prestige, or power to be gained from deciding as a group to claim that Jesus was alive. It just doesn't make any sense to think they did that.

So what does this have to do with these questions you and your friend have been grappling with?

Here's the point you've reached:

It's possible that there's a God. The existence of God doesn't contradict reason or what science tells us about life. In fact, the questions about existence that stubbornly remain — the gaps in what we can say about life, even from a scientific perspective — can very easily point in the direction of a God.

We can even say a few things about this God, based on what we see around us. That God is spirit and the ultimate cause of all that is. God causes and creates with purpose, intention, and design. Humans can know and talk about God, even though we're limited by relatively narrow perception and a definitely tiny vocabulary.

But all of this sets up a whole other set of questions: Who is God, and how does He relate to us as human beings? If I can't measure God, how can I go about knowing Him? And how will I know what I think of as God really *is* God?

Jesus.

Jesus said He was from God. He healed and forgave in God's name. The testimony of those who knew Him — trustworthy people without a dime to be made on this claim — says that after being killed, this Jesus rose again and walked among them.

So...

Jesus must be God, God must be real, and what Jesus says about God is true. That's how we know who God is. He's told us.

No, God doesn't leave us with nothing more than the beauty of the cell, the wonder of the stars, or our own vague yearnings for truth, beauty, and life. He's given us the answers to those questions. Through Jesus, He invites us to listen.

So . . . Our Point Is?

- People have different ideas about everything. That doesn't mean those things don't exist or even have a truth to them that humans beings can't quite grasp.

- The same idea applies to God.

- God can't be just "anything," either. God can't be everything people say about Him, because a lot of those things are contradictory. A lot of people are simply wrong in what they say about God.

- So how do we know the truth about God? Reason can take us only so far. Revelation does the rest — God's told us a lot about Himself.

- That's why Jesus is called the "Word" in the Gospel of John. He's God, directly expressing Himself to us.

- Invite your friend to consider the facts about Jesus, take them seriously with an open mind, and see what she concludes.

So Far...

WE'VE BEEN DEALING with intellectual questions. Things about God that just don't seem to make sense or are hard to understand. These can be big obstacles to faith.

The next set of questions is different, but just as important.

A lot of times people close themselves to God because believers do such rotten things.

They can't trust the message because the messenger is so flawed.

They're also afraid of how taking such a huge step — moving from believing they're on their own in the universe to believing in God who created them, loves them, and to whom they're responsible — will change their lives.

They're distrustful and afraid.

These are hard questions, too, but for a different reason. Here, the witness and actions of the one who's trying to answer are just as important, if not more, than the words they say.

CHAPTER 8

I Don't Believe in God Because...

...There Are So Many Hypocrites in Church.

AND SO YOUR point is . . . what?

There are people who believe in God who don't practice what they preach.

And your point is . . . ?

So . . . what they preach must be false.

Say what? Can you explain exactly how that works?

Your friend probably can't, because if you're brutally logical, you can't avoid the truth that those two ideas — God's existence and the imperfection of those who profess belief — don't have much to do with each other. They can both be true. As a matter of fact, they are. So here's one more case in which pushing is in order. Don't let your friend get away with sloppy thinking or superficial observations. Push. Nicely, but push anyway.

First, take some time to clarify exactly what your friend means by "hypocrite."

"Hypocrisy" is derived from a Greek word, *hypokrisia*, which means "acting." So a real hypocrite is a person who's pretending to be something he's not. She's saying she likes you, then ripping you apart behind your back. He's an anti-pornography crusader who has his own private collection stashed under the bed. He claims diversity and respect for all opinions is really,

really important, but won't let a pro-life commercial run on the television station he manages.

> There's a divinity that shapes our ends,
> Rough-hew them how we will.
> — William Shakespeare, *Hamlet*

Hypocrites, all. Acting one way to conceal their true selves.

If your friend is using the term in this, the proper sense, I'd have to say, and I think you would agree, that churches are not "filled" with these kinds of people. Certainly, there are some. There always have been and there always will be.

But I would imagine that your friend is really talking about the simple reality of believers not fully living up to the ideals of their faith. He's referring to the people who leave church, hop in the cars, and immediately start gossiping about their fellow worshipers, pausing only to cuss out the lady in the white Lincoln who just cut them off.

He might be referring to people he knows who say they believe, go to church, and are even active beyond Sunday morning, but who also (gasp!) sin.

Okay, your friend says, maybe they're not exactly blatant hypocrites, but they aren't very good examples of their faith.

Stop the presses. Of course, they're not perfect exemplars of faith. But few of us are. But, once again, what does our failure have to do with the truth of what we believe? If we always measured the truth of an idea by the perfection or lack of it in the lives of those who follow it, we'd have nothing to believe in.

Your friend probably believes that honesty is a good value to have. She'd rather tell the truth than lie, and she doesn't think cheating or stealing is a good thing to do.

I Don't Believe in God Because...

So has your friend told a few lies in her life? Cheated on homework here and there? Has she ever sneaked some money out of her mom's purse?

Let's hope not, but even if she did, would her failure to live as a totally honest person one hundred percent of the time lead to the conclusion that honesty either doesn't exist or isn't a good value to live by?

This whole line of argument is just an attempt to take an easy way out. If you can find enough faults in the messenger, the theory goes, surely there's something wrong with the message. Right?

No. If you're chatting along these lines, it might be a good time to share with your friend what Catholics believe the Church is. We don't believe it's composed only of saints. We believe that the Church is made up of saints and sinners, bound by faith in Christ, struggling along the road to heaven. We've accepted Jesus' call to follow Him. Sometimes, we fall. Even Peter, the very first pope, failed Jesus in a rather dramatic way — he denied knowing Jesus, not just once, but three times. He was forgiven and continued on the journey.

> Faith is not a thing which one "loses," we merely cease to shape our lives by it.
> — Georges Bernanos, *Diary of a Country Priest*

When we put our faith in Christ, we're entering into a relationship. It's a relationship with the One Who created us, Who knows us, and Who wants us to dwell in love with Him forever. Like in any relationship, we can fail. We can drift away. We can make deliberate choices to betray the friendship. We can let other things become more important. We can even get to a point in which we're just going through the motions, and we have a hard time remembering why we wanted to be in this relationship in the first place.

But — we say it again and again. Does our failure to live up to the promise of something potentially beautiful mean that that something doesn't exist or isn't still worth having?

So . . . Our Point Is?

- Sure, there are people who say they believe in God who fail to live up to the ideals of their faith.

- There are even people who profess those ideals and consciously betray them — those are *real* hypocrites.

- But how does that make what they believe a lie? It says a lot about them, but nothing about the beliefs they say they have.

- You and your friends doubtless hold many ideals and beliefs that you've failed to meet or even betrayed a time or two. That doesn't mean those ideals — honesty, kindness, or loyalty — aren't real or worth living by.

- Simply put: just because believers fail God, that doesn't mean God doesn't exist.

CHAPTER 9

I Don't Believe in God Because...

... People Do Such Horrible Things in the Name of Religion.

THE INQUISITION. SOUTHERN Protestant churches supporting slavery in the United States. Catholics and Protestants slicing, dicing, and burning each other in the Reformation era. Hindus persecuting Sikhs. Never-ending conflict between Muslims and Christians, not to speak of Irish Protestants and Catholics.

All in the name of a god.

This is another pretty serious challenge, but once again, in dealing with it, we have to be rational and tough.

It's a terrible thing to confront, indeed, violence done in the name of God. But, we have to ask, logically speaking, does wrongdoing, even that done by believers for the sake of their belief, invalidate the existence of God?

It's really the same question we asked in the previous chapter, but on a broader scale. There, we were looking at the failure of ordinary believers to live up the ideals of faith in everyday life. Now we're talking about institutional sins, done under the protection of a cross, or a star and crescent, or any other religious symbol one can imagine — for almost every religious group you can think of has, at one time or another, engaged in some sort of activity that ends up depriving people of their rights, freedom, or even their lives.

Does that mean it's all a sham?

Logically speaking, of course, it doesn't, and we'll use the same reasoning we used before to see this. The United States was established under some pretty high ideals. If you don't remember what they are, go back and take a look at the Declaration of Independence and the Constitution. But there have been times in history that those ideals have been misunderstood and even violated. Slavery. Our government's treatment of Native Americans. The placement of Japanese-Americans in relocation camps during World War II. Some would say the dropping of the atomic bomb on the civilian populations of Hiroshima and Nagasaki. Others might point to the tens of millions killed by legalized abortion since 1973.

> The Christian ideal has not been tried and found wanting. It has been found difficult; and left untried.
> — G. K. Chesterton, *What's Wrong with the World*

Horrible things. Most of them were even justified by an appeal to those very ideals so carefully written out in our founding documents, especially the cause of preserving freedom.

So does that make the American experiment in freedom, so unique and foundational in the world's history, not worth pursuing? Do those perversions of freedom render freedom nonexistent?

No. Those evils point out how careful we have to be in defining our ideals and ensuring that we're not letting other agendas blind us to the true nature of those ideals.

Let's turn back to religion. Yes, churches have done some truly awful things, but when you study history carefully, what you'll find is that those deeds, while shielded and justified by words about "God" and "faith," were really about "power," "wealth," and "greed."

It's just a basic — admittedly, very frustrating — reality. People use religion for their own selfish ends. People also can act out of terribly mixed motives and honestly come to believe that their lust for earthly power or domination is actually justified by faith.

Ask your friend about the mixed motives in his own life. When he does well in school, is it always and every time for the pure motive of pursuing knowledge and developing his mind? Does he sometimes do it to keep his parents off his back? Might he sometimes perform well for the sake of his own pride?

Look at it another way. I wouldn't be surprised if one of your friend's (and yours as well) personal ideals is to "be himself," and there's nothing wrong with that. It's actually one of the things you're supposed to do with the unique life you've been given, and it's not a terribly bad ideal to live by — as long as it's coupled with a few others that aren't quite so self-centered.

But have you ever done things in the name of "being yourself" that were really rotten? Or actually even in conflict with the goal of being your real, best self? I'll bet you can think of a few. The drive to be what we think is "ourselves" can lead us to stupidity and even worse.

Your friend needs to understand, once again, what the Church is. Jesus told us that He'd be with us always. Catholic Christians have always interpreted that to mean that the core of what Jesus wants us to do in His name — teach the truth about God, heal, love, and forgive as He did — remains safe. But the fact remains that Jesus' mandate is carried out by flawed, and sometimes even willfully blind and sinful, human beings who've been known to use the Church to construct systems that oppress rather than bring people to the liberating love of God.

It's happened before, and it will, unfortunately, happen again. You don't do the truth any service if you deny the tragedy of the

Church getting itself in positions in which the greed for power and wealth blind it to the Gospel.

But take care to point out the following to your friend:

Such things have never happened to the whole Church. These events and eras come and go. They're never permanent.

At the times in which segments of the Church have fallen to the temptation to using God's name to harm or exploit, there have always been prophetic voices pointing out the wrong. And in the end, those voices, small and persistent, always win, because truth does.

Secondly, it's not as if the Church *claims* to be free from sin on earth, either for itself as a whole or as a mark of baptism. If it did, the argument that the Church had done horrible things would have more weight. But when you think about it, the whole *point* of Christianity is that Jesus redeems us — saves us — in our sinfulness. We are loved and forgiven despite our unworthiness; despite our pride, arrogance, and frequency of missing the point.

I Don't Believe in God Because...

(And as I keep saying... that's why we call it *Good News*.)

Here's the way God works through the Church: not by showing the world our own earthly perfection, but by showing how great, loving, and merciful *God* is, as He holds us up, forgives, and works in His amazing, loving, and merciful ways through the Body of Christ.

Because any harm done by so-called believers in God's name has been far outweighed by the good done by the Church in that same God's name. If your friend has any sense of history, he should understand that there's no other single institution that's provided more health care, education, or aid to the poor through world history than the Catholic Church. None. Hundreds of millions of people have found peace, fulfillment, and strength through relationships with the God they've learned about through the Church's teaching and preaching and had nourished through the sacraments.

Let us forgive and ask forgiveness! While we praise God who, in his merciful love, has produced in the Church a wonderful harvest of holiness, missionary zeal, total dedication to Christ and neighbor, we cannot fail to recognize *the infidelities to the Gospel committed by some of our brethren*, especially during the second millennium. Let us ask pardon for the divisions which have occurred among Christians, for the violence some have used in the service of the truth and for the distrustful and hostile attitudes taken towards the followers of other religions.

We humbly ask forgiveness for the part which each of us has had in these evils by our own actions, thus helping to disfigure the face of the Church.

— Pope John Paul II, Homily, March 12, 2000

Okay. There's no arguing that bad things have been done in the name of God.

Any fool can look in the Scriptures and read the truth about what God intended us to be and what Jesus makes possible through His presence in our midst. That same fool can see that the misuse of religion for evil ends conflicts with that message.

So whose fault is that?

So . . . Our Point Is?

- Logic. Always logic. Don't let emotion rule the day here.

- If people misuse a belief to justify wrongdoing, does that mean the belief is wrong? No.

- The Christian Church has certainly been guilty of sin and the betrayal of Jesus' teaching, but never completely. There have always been voices calling for truth, and with time, the Church always admits mistakes that have been made.

- The problem is never the belief — it's the greed, pride, and arrogance that lead people to misuse the belief.

- We all do the same thing in our individual lives. We all are guilty, at least some time in our lives, of using ideals to conceal and justify wrongdoing.

CHAPTER 10

I Don't Believe in God Because...

...It's What I Believe and I Don't Need Anyone Else to Tell Me What to Believe.

SUPPOSE SOMEONE ASKED you to construct a bridge. Solve a problem in astrophysics. Conjugate some Japanese verbs.

Or just suppose someone asked you to make a rhubarb pie.

Would you nod, ask for a minute to yourself, and announce, "Sure thing. But just let me take some time to ponder what's inside me so I can know what to do. No, no thanks, but I don't need the cookbook. Keep the engineering texts. I can figure it out from what my heart is telling me."

How dumb would that be, exactly?

Why is it any different with spiritual matters?

Why do we imagine that, when it comes to life decisions and knowledge about God, outside information and the experience of others is useless?

Why do we imagine each of our teenaged selves to be some store of infallible, unquestioned wisdom when it comes to God, religion, and morality?

I suppose part of the reason has to do with these trends we've been coming back to over and over again in this book. Because a lot of people say they believe truth about such matters is subjective and relative (although we're pretty sure they don't really and truly believe that — remember, you can talk relativism, but no one really lives it), and because we're so stuck on the idea that the only "truth" is that which is scientifically demonstrable and everything else is up for grabs, we've fallen into this big, muddy, sticky hole. We think that the great questions of existence that a lot of smart people have contemplated and written eloquently about don't require any actual thought or knowledge to grapple with meaningfully.

How can that be?

Could you imagine, even for a second, walking into the first day your calculus class and announcing, "Hey, teacher, thanks for trying, but there's really nothing you can teach me. Go ahead and give me the final now."

Of course not.

Questions of God and the nature of ultimate reality and meaning have occupied far more minds and hearts than scientific questions through history. How could one teenager living at one tiny point in time in human history have all the answers? And, more importantly, how could that teenager believe that the experiences and ideas of the thousands of people who've led spiritual journeys themselves are totally useless to his own search? How arrogant is that?

> God is not what you imagine or what you think you understand. If you understand, you have failed.
> — St. Augustine of Hippo, *De Trinitate*

As you can see, this objection isn't directly focused on that specific question of God's existence. It's more an expression of an obstacle your friend is placing in the path of serious thought. Why do people do that?

A lot of reasons. Some people are truly just arrogant jerks who don't think they can be told anything by anyone. They're patiently waiting to be through with school so they can run the world. There's not much you can do about that but pray they survive with some self-worth intact on the day after the inevitable humiliating revelation of their equality with the rest of this struggling, half-seeing, constant screw-up we call the human race.

Some are just lazy — or just believe that spiritual matters are, indeed, this big squishy cumulous cloud of fantasies and ideas that has no permanent shape, that looks like anything you want it to.

"Hey! Look, it's God! What can you see?"

"Cool. I think I see a really huge mother bear who just wants to hug me all the time."

"Whoa. From here it looks like a little guy with a beard handing out flowers."

"Whatever."

To deal with this, go back to that chapter on truth. If God is, God can't be everything and anything.

But you already know there's something else, right? Because you know yourself, and you remember all the times you've waved away your parents' and teachers' advice, knowing in your heart of hearts that you know what's best for yourself, and heck if you're going to listen to the words of old people who "don't know what it's like to be young today."

> Anyone who wants to be cured of ignorance must confess it.
> — Montaigne, *Essays*

Yes, at the root of this blow-off of thousands of years of wisdom lies the gut instinct that seeds every teenage blow-off of adult life.

"No one is going to tell ME what to do!"

 I Don't Believe in God Because...

Right?

So before you take this on as it comes from your friend's mouth, take a breath and think about yourself. Deal humbly with your friend, because you know you've probably turned your back on the wisdom of the ages plenty of times.

Just encourage your friend to think in these terms:

It's hard to admit sometimes, but we have to be honest. We're teenagers. Young adults who think the way that young adults really are supposed to think. We're supposed to be idealistic and energetic about our power and opportunities to change the world. There's nothing wrong with that.

But there's a problem with being convinced we have all the answers and that no one of the millions of people who've walked the planet before us has anything interesting to say or anything wise to teach us. Sure, the world changes all the time, and the language previous generations have used to talk about the big questions may be difficult to understand, but that doesn't mean their words aren't worthy of attention. After all, language, customs, and even ways of thinking change, but human nature doesn't. That's why people still read Genesis, Homer, and Shakespeare. There's truth there — reflections on experience that are good to hear.

Invite your friend to just honestly contemplate this question, and then drop it, and move on to something else, like the ballgame this weekend. Literally hundreds of millions of people have believed in God and many have written about their experiences and lives of faith. How can you so easily dismiss that and celebrate the limited ideas of a twenty-first century young person as being superior and in no need at all of any of the wisdom of the past?

Oh, yes. You might ponder that question yourself, too.

So . . . Our Point Is?

- We're not born full of knowledge about anything.

- It's absurd to think that no one else has anything interesting or helpful to tell us about God.

- It doesn't make sense — if we're complaining that we have difficulty understanding God, why would we reject the insights that others have had before us? Wouldn't it make more sense to welcome that wisdom?

CHAPTER 11

I Don't Believe in God Because...

...I Want to Be Free to Be Myself.

YOUR FRIEND DOESN'T have a bad goal — to be herself. After all, it would be pretty strange and disturbing to want to be another person.

But when you hear this objection — that belief in God would somehow make her into someone else — you need to ask a couple of questions yourself.

The first, and most important, one is why is she making God the Bad Guy here?

Why would faith in God threaten her sense of her own identity?

It might have something to do with exactly who she thinks God is.

Have you noticed how many times in the course of this book, we've had to address objections to God's existence by clearing up exactly who God is?

I wouldn't be surprised if this is just one more example.

The best way to answer this question would probably be in a very personal way, because it deals with personal issues. No one can explain this to your friend better than you can. A faith relationship with God is the exact opposite of confining: Through God's eyes, you can see who you really are.

If you need help in talking about this to your friend, think about the following points.

Who is God, anyway? Is your friend operating out of the assumption that God is some hostile force Who created her just to make her miserable? Who gave her free will just to see her squirm under an endless stream of divine prohibitions?

Where in the world did that come from? Push your friend on this. What's she basing that concept of God on? The words of Jesus, Who talks about God's love and forgiveness, and Who ate with outcasts and sinners? From the endless stories in the Old Testament of God's constant faithfulness and forgiveness, even when the Israelites turned their backs on Him again and again? Where?

Point out to your friend that if she's refusing to believe in God because she thinks God wants her to be unhappy and doesn't have her best interests at heart, then she's absolutely right. That's not God. She's basing her fears on something that doesn't even exist.

Go back to the question of who God is — the Creator who made each one of us, individually, in His own image — that is, like Him in our freedom, and our ability to love, know, and create. That means He created each of us on purpose, that there are no accidental people in God's plan. He created each of us — you, your friend — out of passionate love because He wanted you to exist and be yourself. No one else. Yourself.

> I live and love in God's peculiar light.
> — Michelangelo

That's God. Not some fantasy based on cartoons or rooted in deep-seated childhood fears of punishment.

You can't say much more than that, except once more to invite your friend to take a look at the Scriptures herself. To listen to and consider the prayers that Catholics address to this horrible figure who's out to strip His creation of its uniqueness and individuality — like that makes any sense at all.

I Don't Believe in God Because...

(And if you don't know where to begin with this, well, just start simply. Go take a look at Mark's Gospel. It's really short — only sixteen chapters — and go through it with your friend. Who's God, really? Who are we? Any week you choose, you'll find the germ of an answer there.)

If your friend is agreeable, you might engage in a little discussion about what she means by "being herself" here in the dawn of the twenty-first century. Where exactly does she get her ideas about what "being herself" means?

If she's like a lot of people, after some honest reflection, she'll be surprised to see how much of what she values in the name of "being herself" is really dictated to her by outside forces.

Does being herself mean making a lot of money and getting a lot of stuff? Where does she get the idea that all of that will make her happy? Push and dig here. Where in the world does that come from? From the reality of a world in which wealthy people are just as miserable as the poorest of the poor, if not more so? From looking at the lives of those who focus on material gain and are never, ever fully satisfied, since there's always more to get?

Or has she been brainwashed by corporations who've convinced her she needs stuff, from cars to cool clothes to amazingly expensive shoes, to be happy so (here's the big news) they can make more profit?

Where's the freedom to be herself there?

Does being herself mean being sexually irresponsible? Let's do some more thinking. Does that kind of behavior really bring freedom? Or is it just more enslavement — to the idea that your self-worth depends on your sexual appeal or experience? Does sexual "freedom" really free us, or does it enclose us in ever more limiting boxes of fear as we wonder what diseases we might have, worry every month if we are or have made someone pregnant, wonder if the person we're with really likes us for who we are, and, in the end, wonder what value this gift will have left when we find someone we want to share it with for the rest of our lives?

That's freedom? To be ourselves?

Sounds like enslavement to me, enslavement to this big lie, revolutionary and unique to our time — that sex is a meaningless act of pure recreation. What's the evidence that this assertion is true? Don't the broken hearts scattered on the battlefield and preponderance of nineteen-year old romantic cynics hint that it might be a lie?

We could go on, but you can probably think of a lot more examples that make the point. More often than not, the moment when we most proclaim our right and desire to be "free to be ourselves" are also the times in which we're most deeply enslaved to our pride, our sins, or our culture.

Faith in God — real loving, trusting friendship — is the opposite. It's interesting that when you read accounts of conversion experiences from St. Paul to the present day, you never, ever find someone claiming, "Oh my, I feel so limited and chained now that I believe in God. Fantastic!"

> When we find the truth that shapes our lives we have found more than an idea. We have found a Person. We have come upon the actions of One Who is still hidden, but Whose work proclaims Him holy and worthy to be adored. And in Him we also find ourselves.
> — Thomas Merton, *No Man Is an Island*

Not at all. In fact, conversion stories unfailingly convey the opposite feeling — freedom. When people come to believe and deeply accept the existence and love of God, they feel free. How can that be?

Because real faith in the true God means understanding God's true nature and relation to you: God made you. He made you on purpose, in His image, to love and be loved. You are who He made you to be, not what anyone else tells you that you should be. The closer you are to God, the better you can understand Him and, consequently yourself.

It's real freedom.

If we let Christ into our lives, we lose nothing, nothing, absolutely nothing of what makes life free, beautiful and great. No! Only in this friendship are the doors of life opened wide. Only in this friendship is the great potential of human existence truly revealed. Only in this friendship do we experience beauty and liberation. And so, today, with great strength and great conviction, on the basis of long personal experience of life, I say to you, dear young people: Do not be afraid of Christ! He takes nothing away, and he gives you everything. When we give ourselves to him, we receive a hundredfold in return. Yes, open, open wide the doors to Christ — and you will find true life.

— Pope Benedict XVI[2]

So you can see that the impact of the answer to this question, more than any of the others, weighs on you. If you experience faith as a confining burden, you're not going to have much to say. And if that's the case, maybe this chapter really wasn't for your friend. Maybe it was really for you.

---

[2] http://www.vatican.va/holy_father/benedict_xvi/homilies/documents/hf_ben-xvi_hom_20050424_inisio-pontificato_en.html.

So ... Our Point Is?

- So, you want to be yourself. Good. Who are you, anyway? Where did you come from? Where are you going?

- Most of the time when people want to "be themselves," they end up enslaved to something else.

- A faith relationship with God offers freedom, because when we see ourselves through God's eyes, we see ourselves as we really are. When we believe that God believes in us, we're free to be that person without fear.

- Your friend should be invited to read personal accounts of people who've come to have faith in God. She'll find that in every case, turning one's life over to God gives a sense of freedom, confidence, and possibility, not imprisonment.

CHAPTER 12

I Don't Believe in God Because...

... I Don't Need Him.

WE'VE BEEN WORKING pretty hard, haven't we? Are you tired yet?

It's okay. Thinking brilliant thoughts about the Meaning of Life will do that to you.

I hate to tell you, but we're not done yet.

There are just a few more questions to deal with. You hear them a lot, but none of them is really quite huge enough to deserve its very own chapter, so we'll just throw them all together in a little heap:

> ***Religion is a crutch for people who aren't strong enough to deal with life.***

Yes. That's it.

Moses. Jesus of Nazareth. St. Paul. Mother Teresa. Martin Luther King, Jr. Mahatma Gandhi. Pope John Paul II.

What a bunch of wimps.

Anything in life can be a crutch, if you use it that way. Sports, academic success, work, music, even family. If we're weak people, we can hide behind anything, refusing to deal with our fears and emptiness.

Religion isn't unique that way.

But if the fact that religion can be used as a crutch makes it one, then everything else in life is a crutch, too. We know that's not true.

No, religion isn't a crutch. It's an answer to the most important questions that people ask.

And what takes more strength? Seeking the answers to those questions or avoiding them?

Who's the escapist now?

People without religion can be good. They can be happy, too.

True. There are plenty of nice unbelievers walking the planet in states of general contentment and even occasional joy. No argument there.

But . . . (If you would like to count the number of times I use that particular word in this book, you're welcome to. I'll send you a piece of gum or something if you let me know.)

But . . .

Emotion doesn't always correlate to the truth. There have probably been plenty of times you've experienced "happiness" doing something that was wrong. You might also have had enough experience to go through times in which you think, "It can't get better than this," and a few years later... it does. You grow into another stage of life and different ways of thinking that bring more — maybe even deeper — joy.

My point is this: How do we know that the happy unbeliever wouldn't be even happier if he let God into his life? How do we know that the already basically moral unbeliever wouldn't be even better if she lived out of a faith relationship with God?

You could say the same thing about those rotten religious hypocrites we talked about a few chapters ago. Who's to say their sins wouldn't be unbearably, destructively worse if they

I Don't Believe in God Because...

didn't have what sliver of faith they have keeping them from sliding over into total repulsiveness?

Back to the happy unbeliever. Most of those people aren't deep-seated, virulent, principled atheists, anyway. Most of them believe that there's meaning in life, purpose, and a basic set of shared moral values we need to live by in order to be content. As I've pointed out several times, those people's belief in some kind of transcendent meaning is really just a few steps from God, once they see that it's impossible to have any such thing without God.

> God can be denied only on the surface; but he cannot be denied where human experience reaches down beneath the surface of flat, vapid, commonplace existence.
> — Nicholas Berdyaev, *Dream and Reality*

A little bit of open-minded reading will reveal, however, that people who are deeply spiritual and have intimate, loving friendships with God aren't just "happy." There's a joy and peace in their lives that you just don't find in any other kind of person.

So — you should ask — why settle for happiness, when joy is possible?

All that matters in life is believing something, and being sincere in what you believe.

By this time, you should be so incredibly smart about all this stuff, that you don't even need me to tell you how dumb that statement is. But in case you're unsure, I'll help you out anyway.

That's silly. So there's no difference in living your life according to the values of the KKK and the teachings of Jesus. A sincere Nazi is leading a life of as much integrity as the Dalai Lama.

Because, you know, they're both really sincere.

... I Don't Need Him.

Please. Ideas and values are important. Here's why:

First of all, the truth is important. It's vital. Think about how you'd feel if you were dating someone, and after six months, she told you, "You know what? I don't really like you. I was just going out with you to make Biff over there jealous, and it worked. Thanks for everything. See ya!"

> In the opinion that there is a God, there are difficulties; but in the contrary opinion, there are absurdities.
> — Voltaire, *Traité de Metaphysique*

Would the fact that you'd had some enjoyable times, seen some good movies, and, for a while, were "happy" be any consolation at all? No. You'd be mad because you'd bought a lie. You'd feel as if you wasted your time, when you could have been spending your time pursuing something real.

It's true with all those relatively minor things in life: We don't want to live according to lies. We want to live honestly and in reality.

Why would anyone be content with living according to a lie about the meaning and purpose of life? Shouldn't reality and truth count there, too?

I Don't Believe in God Because...

CHAPTER 13

I Don't Believe in God Because...

...Innocent People Suffer.

FINALLY.

This may be the last question in our journey, but not because it's the least important.

After all, remember what Jesus said? "The first shall be last"? That's sort of what's going on here. I've got this question last precisely because it is the most important and persistent challenge, not only to the existence of God, period, but to everything we say God is: loving, powerful, and the One in charge.

It's pretty simple, really.

You say God exists, and He's all-powerful and all-good.

Then why do innocent people suffer?

We're not talking about the suffering that comes from the harm human beings purposefully inflict on one another — the abuse, the meanness, the crime. That's not so hard to understand.

We're talking about babies with leukemia. We're talking about young mothers dropping dead from a stroke and leaving uncomprehending families behind. We're talking about the bewildering mysteries of mental illness. We're talking about the Holocaust, in which God's chosen were chosen by pure evil for destruction and unimaginable suffering.

How in the world can we even pretend a loving God exists in the face of such horror? Where do we get the nerve?

It's not an easy question, and no one on earth has ever emerged from wrestling with it with a simple, pat answer.

So what is there left to say? Does all of our faith, our conviction about God's existence, presence, and mercy, fall down flat and empty in the face of the darkness of suffering?

There are many ways to approach this very tough issue, but this is the way I'd suggest you go about it when you're asked:

First, remind your friend, once again, that he's not the first person to wonder about this. He may get tired of hearing you say this, but that doesn't matter. Too often, young people believe that their questions are totally unique. They need to know that it just isn't so. The question of God and suffering is as old as all rational thought. Philosophers even have a name for it — *theodicy*. Ever since human beings have discerned the Caring, Powerful Presence that lies beyond visible reality, they've immediately been moved to ask, "I know You're there — why does it seem sometimes that You're not? Why are You allowing my child to suffer? Why won't You make it rain? Why is it raining so much? Why does evil seem to have so much power?"

As we've said, philosophers and theologians of every faith have had a lot to say about the matter over the past few millennia. To get a sense of this, just go to the Internet and do a search for "theodicy," or "God and evil." You'll be busy for a long time, and you might learn something in between times your brain's not threatening to explode from the wealth of ideas on the subject. For right now, the best we can do is focus on three points:

God doesn't cause evil. Genesis tells us that God created a good, harmonious world. Sin and the resultant suffering were introduced by human choices. As mysterious as it might seem, even physical suffering is related to this sinful disharmony, and none of it — the hurt, the pain, or the evil we cause one

I Don't Believe in God Because...

another — is what God wants. Jesus makes this clear over and over. When confronted with sickness, Jesus doesn't say, "Hey, deal with it. Must be God's will." Nope. He heals. He fixes. He makes it clear that God's will is for our wholeness and healing.

So . . . God doesn't cause evil. God enters into the world He created, and we messed up, over and over again, constantly in fact, to heal our brokenness. That's the essential story the Bible tells — not the common misconception that Judaism and Christianity is about human beings doing fine and being constantly invaded by a God who wants to put an end to the fun. No, it's about God giving us everything — most importantly, natures that are in His image and capable of deep joy, peace, and love — and those same human beings screwing it up by being selfish, power-mad, greedy, and proud . . . then God patiently trying, over and over again, to point us in the right direction and say, "I love you. Figure out who you are and live that way."

God doesn't cause evil, doesn't want it, and is always near, offering us the good news about what will bring us peace, if we only listen.

Secondly, who suffers and why is a mystery.

Remember Job? We talked about him at the beginning of this book, so it's fitting that we meet him again near the end. You remember that Job is a man who has everything he could possibly want and loses it for no apparent reason. In those days, most people believed that God blessed the virtuous with material wealth and health, and that the reverse was also true: Poverty and illness were punishment.

The writer of Job, whoever this genius was, took this simple story and wrote an amazingly profound work of poetry that stood as a direct — even radical — challenge to those assumptions about blessings and curses.

You remember that when Job's friends come to help him out, they get fixated on what he must have done wrong. Because,

you see, he *must* have done something wrong to bring God's wrath down on him in this intense way.

But Job is stubborn. Sitting there on the ashes of his life, covered with boils, Job insists that he has been a good man, and whatever wrong he's done in his life has surely not been serious enough to bring this kind of wrath down on him.

So Job and his friends argue, until finally Job gets so frustrated with their foolish answers and the whole situation that he decides to take the courageous and even foolhardy step of risking his own life to confront God Himself with his question:

"This is my final plea; let the Almighty answer me!" (Job 31:38).

And what happens?

God does answer — out of a "whirlwind" He speaks to Job. The words of God flow like a tremendous river of poetry, taking in the whole of His works and mysterious purposes, which are, the point is, far beyond the power of any human being to comprehend:

"Where were you when I founded the earth? Tell me, if you have understanding" (Job 38:4).

It may seem harsh, and even like a divine blow-off, but it's not. Go read it yourself and see. The (literally) inspired writer of Job is making the point that every single attempt to explain questions of theodicy comes back to: It's a mystery. Suffering is not God's doing, but since the world belongs to Him, He weaves it into His purpose.

There are a lot of other points to be made on this score, all of which you should bring up: God created us as free creatures. The risk of that freedom is the ability to make choices for evil. But if our freedom couldn't go in that direction, it wouldn't be real, and we wouldn't be free; we wouldn't be human, either. The choice to love isn't of much value at all when it's not really a choice. To constantly interfere with our exercise of our freedom would render us less than human.

So, our second point is simple and unarguable: God's allowance of the evil that results from our sin isn't inconsistent with His goodness. He created us to be free, and to interfere with that would violate our integrity.

The third point is the most "Christian" of them all. Your friend might not even be faintly interested in Christianity, but he needs to hear this. It's the element of our faith that truly sets it apart from every other world. It addresses the issue head-on, but in a startling way: not with words, but with a person.

Remember where we are in this discussion: We've acknowledged that God doesn't will evil at all. He created the world to be an expression of Himself, just as any artist views his or her creation: harmonious, inhabited by creatures made in His image, free to love and create even more beauty.

But evil entered the world and continues to roam it, causing pain and suffering, injustice and oppression, broken hearts, bodies, and spirits. God can't violate our freedom by giving us a magic fix, but He's among us constantly, reminding us of the way back to peace and giving us the strength to start walking. That's the story of the Bible and the Church.

There's something else, though. Since God not only loves, but is Love, He wants to do what any lover does: He wants to be joined with those He loves, to experience what they experience, to take on their joy, and even their pain.

Ask any parent. When confronted with the sight of their child in pain, most parents, given the chance, would trade places with that child. Without even thinking twice, they'd take on their child's suffering.

So how could God do this? How could God conquer the evil that's infected His creation without violating the precious freedom of His creatures?

...Innocent People Suffer.

He could become one of them.

His name is Jesus.

Jesus, born of a woman, growing to teach, preach, and heal. Jesus, miraculously, mysteriously both God and man, Who showed us Who He was without doubt when He rose from the dead.

But remember, before He rose from the dead, He hung from a cross.

Unjustly convicted, viciously beaten, stripped, and nailed through wrists and ankles in front of jeering crowds who shouted at Him words that sound suspiciously like the question we've been asking:

They asked Him, if He was who He said he was, why couldn't He stop the suffering?

If He was God, why was evil still at work?

(Jesus...)

Who, though he was in the form of God, did not regard equality with God something to be grasped.

Rather, he emptied himself, taking the form of a slave, coming in human likeness; and found human in appearance,

he humbled himself, becoming obedient to death, even death on a cross.

Because of this, God greatly exalted him and bestowed on him the name that is above every name,

that at the name of Jesus every knee should bend, of those in heaven and on earth and under the earth,

and every tongue confess that Jesus Christ is LORD.
— Philippians 2:6-11

The answer was a while in coming. Three days, to be exact. But it was all the answer any of us could ask for: Not in words, but in presence.

Alive. Jesus, God-made-victim of sin and death, alive. They could not hold Him, they could not win.

Do you see?

Christianity isn't about rules, no matter what your friend wants to think. It's not about nice teachings from a nice man. It's about God coming into this world to re-create His creation, to twist it all back around to its rightful place, turn the world's expectations upside-down, and give us another chance.

So, your friend says. That's great. But 2,000 years later, there's still sin. There's still horrible evil.

Okay, you say, there's no denying that. But whose fault is that?

Look at what Jesus said and did. Look at the kind of life of wholeness and healing He invites us to. Would the world — would our lives — be in such a mess if we just listened?

Of course not.

So here's the final answer to this question: It's not a justification, a pat, neat, logical syllogism or even a proof. It's a man.

God suffers with us. God eventually rescues us from suffering and evil. God will prevail.

It may not be what your questioning friend is looking for, since it's not neat, scientific, or provable. But it's real. Consider the times you've suffered, perhaps from a serious illness or tragedy. What helps at those times? People sitting around chatting, explaining why everything's happened and assuring you, very reasonably, that you'll feel better tomorrow?

I wouldn't be surprised if you, like Job, just wanted all of those people to shut up and go away. Rationalizations of what you were going through didn't help. What gave you comfort was Presence. The Presence in your life Who knew that words could only do so much, but Who loved you enough to just be with you.

At the end, after he's encountered God, Job says:

"I had heard of you by word of mouth, but now my eye has seen you" (42:5).

These are words we can repeat in the midst of our own suffering, as a prayer, when we keep our eyes on the Cross and the God who is willing to suffer.

That's the place we find peace. That's the Person who gives us hope. That's the One Who loves us in and through everything — the good, the bad, the joy, and the pain of being human.

The LORD took his wounds with him to eternity. He is a wounded God; he let himself be injured through his love for us. His wounds are a sign for us that he understands and allows himself to be wounded out of love for us.

— Pope Benedict XVI[3]

So . . . Our Point Is?

- Evil is real. It stands in opposition to good, and actively seeks to bring us sorrow, disharmony, and suffering. Evil doesn't want good to happen.

- God didn't cause evil, but because He respects the freedom and integrity of what He has made, He permits it.

- God is constantly present to us, giving us the strength and grace to resist evil and make sense of life.

- God entered the world as one of us, and has suffered with us.

- Our answer to the question of God and suffering is Jesus crucified and risen. God shares our suffering, and overcomes it.

---

[3] http://www.zenit.org/article-19428?1=English.

...Innocent People Suffer.

EPILOGUE

What's the Alternative?

NASTY, BRUTISH, AND SHORT.

That's the way an eighteenth-century philosopher, Thomas Hobbes, described life.

Without God, that pretty well sums it up.

Your friend may want to deny God's existence. She may work really hard to convince herself and you that such a thing — a loving Creator God who made and sustains us — just isn't possible, and that such an idea is nothing more than a pathetic, hopeful illusion.

But what is a world without God?

No smart remarks about getting to sleep late on Sundays are allowed here. We're getting to the end of this very long, convoluted road now, and we can't stop pushing. Pushing for honesty and clear-headedness.

Here's what it comes down to:

If there is no God, there is no meaning to life. At all. It's just not possible.

All we have then is nature and what it produces. That blind, cold, unfeeling nature that brings things to birth, watches them decay, and absorbs them right back up again.

Nature doesn't produce meaning. It only produces itself.

No God — no meaning.

Without God, there's no such thing as objective standards of right and wrong.

To wish there should be no God is to wish that things which we love and strive to realize and make permanent, should be only temporary and doomed to destruction.
— W. P. Montague, *Belief Unbound*

God is at the heart of morality. Without God, we all have permission to make up our own rules, and in that case, there's no standard of judgment — there's only might.

Whoever has the most power gets to set the rules.

Fyodor Dostoyevsky, the great Russian novelist, put it best: "Without God," he said, "everything is permitted."

Think about it. What happens when human beings throw off transcendent meaning and objective values?

Auschwitz. The Gulag. Columbine.

That's what happens.

Here's the point: A world without God is a world without meaning and value. There's no reason to do anything except live totally for yourself. But remember — since there's no Absolute — you don't have the right to get mad, then, when someone else's desires threaten your desires, or even your life.

You've dispensed with God. What "standard" do you have to appeal to?

Do you see how absurd that is?

As I stated before, I don't think any of your friends who claims to be an atheist is a hard-core unbeliever. Why? Because I've no doubt he does, in his heart, assume the existence of meaning and purpose in life, as well as broad absolute moral standards.

How cool would it be if you could help him see the short but necessary path from what he already believes to the joy and peace of a relationship with the living God of love and life?

Can you think of a greater gift that a friend could ever offer?

Our hearts are restless until they rest in Thee, O LORD.
— St. Augustine of Hippo, *Confessions*

For Further Reading

(*Tough stuff, but worth it)

General Apologetics and Faith

Mere Christianity by C. S. Lewis

Fundamentals of the Faith by Peter Kreeft

Handbook of Catholic Apologetics: Reasoned Answers to Questions of Faith by Peter Kreeft and Ronald Tacelli

Why Christian? by Douglas John Hall

Theology and Sanity by Frank J. Sheed

The Yes of Jesus Christ by Pope Benedict XVI

Catechism of the Catholic Church

Science and God

The Language of God: A Scientist Presents Evidence for Belief by Francis Collins

God: the Evidence by Patrick Glynn

*God and the New Physics by Paul Davies

God and the Astronomers by Robert Jastrow

God and Suffering

The Problem of Pain by C. S. Lewis

Personal Stories and Reflections

Confessions by St. Augustine of Hippo

Pensées by Blaise Pascal

The Long Loneliness by Dorothy Day

The Seven Storey Mountain by Thomas Merton

Notes

Notes

Notes

Notes

Notes